More laughs from
A TREASURY OF HUMOR
on...

BUSINESS
The chairman of a bank reported to the officers
and staff members that the institution was "on
the brink." The next year, however, he said he
was glad to inform them that the bank "has taken
a step forward."

HISTORY
A reporter asked Mahatma Gandhi (1869–
1948), "What do you think of Western civilization?" Gandhi replied, "I think it would be a
good idea."

ON MONEY
A young man took his girlfriend out to a restaurant. After the meal he was studying the bill at
some length, and his girl observed him with concern. "Gary," she asked, "you look sick. Is it
something I ate?"

Also by Eric W. Johnson
Published by Ivy Books:

A TREASURY OF HUMOR II

A
TREASURY
OF
HUMOR

An Indexed Collection of Anecdotes

Eric W. Johnson

IVY BOOKS • NEW YORK

Ivy Books
Published by Ballantine Books
Copyright © 1989 by Eric W. Johnson

Library of Congress Catalog Card Number: 89-60195

ISBN 0-8041-0587-1

This edition published by arrangement with Prometheus Books

Manufactured in the United States of America

First Ballantine Books Edition: December 1990

15 14 13 12

An Osmotic Table of Contents

I label this Table of Contents "osmotic" because it is impossible cleanly, neatly, and dryly to categorize humorous stories into chapters. Stories in almost any life-subject category can be used to illustrate and illuminate many other aspects of life.

Osmosis is the passage of fluid through a thin membrane. And so the living fluid of humor in these stories will tend to move through the membranes of chapter separations. That's the way life is. Politics osmotifies into Religion, Religion into Schools (illegally?), Schools into Language, Language into Sex, Sex into Problems of Life, and much of all of the above into Old Age, Children, Fund-Raising, and Family Life. Therefore, if you want to find stories about a given aspect of life—whether it be efficiency experts, condoms, Quakers, teeth, threats, or love, etc.—look in the index.

How to Use This Book
Again and Again

You probably aren't going to read this book straight through, although it flows and you might. It's probably more enjoyable in half-hour stretches while waiting for dinner (even if you're cooking it) or a night's sleep, or while fending off TV. Or, you might dip into the book looking for a story to illustrate a point, to jazz up a speech, or even to win an argument. Whatever your purpose, you will be helped by the index—probably the longest you have ever encountered in a book with less than 250 pages of text, even a heavy academic work. The index combines into a single listing entries of two sorts:

There are *identification entries*, which enable you to locate again a story you have read and enjoyed, and now or later want to use or tell. For example, the two stories in the introduction are identification-indexed as:

rabbit in Altoona, 2
seagull dropping/toilet paper, 1

And there are *subject entries*, which enable you to find stories on a subject you might need to talk or write about. For example, the rabbit (2) and seagull (1) stories in the introduction are subject–indexed as:

The numbers after the index entries refer to the *number* of the story, not the page the story is on. Glance at the index now and see how it works.

Introduction

I have been collecting funny stories for about forty years as a husband, a parent, a schoolteacher, an administrator, an advisor to schools, and while writing 44 books, some of which have been remaindered and others—the ultimate humiliation—*shredded*. I have used these stories in speeches and workshops, as well as at parties and other gatherings. I've tried a lot of them out on my wife, with whom, in spite of or perhaps because of this, I still live joyously. There is no item in this book that has not gotten a laugh, a chuckle, or a wry smile of delight.

Before I started to write this book, I read a score or more of works on humor, and also several collections with titles like *4800 Jokes for All Occasions*. For the most part, I found them dull. But the dullest reading in the world is the "analysis" of humor, whether by psychiatrists, ministers, sociologists, or even humorists. As E. B. White said, it's something like dissecting a frog. "It's very bad for the frog." To which Robert Benchley added, "By the time you have 'humor' analyzed, it will be found that the necessity for laughing has been relieved." So I vowed to write this book, or collect this collection, without attempting to "interpret" humor.

What sorts of people will find the book useful and pleasing?

* anyone who wants to be entertaining
* anyone who wants to be entertained
* anyone who wants to make a point memorably
* anyone who wants to spice up a conversation
* anyone who wants to enjoy marriage more
* conference speakers
* teachers
* preachers
* lawyers
* lecturers
* doctors
* party-goers
* before/during/after–dinner speakers
* and anyone who enjoys the orgasmic pleasure of leading up to a laugh and then hearing it burst forth

One big problem about publishing humorous stories: they circulate freely, untrappable by copyright laws. After all, when something funny is said or written, enjoyed, and told and retold, who knows where it will go from there? This is illustrated by our first story.

1. Two supposedly senile men were committed to an institutional home near the sea. They were taken out one morning for a walk, accompanied by an attendant, Albert. As they strolled along the shore, a seagull flew low and dropped a blob of excrement, which landed right on top of the bald head of one of the elders. Albert saw what happened and said in great concern, "Wait right here. I'll get some toilet paper."

As the attendant ran toward the building, one elder turned to the other, pointed toward Albert, and said, "He's a darned fool. That seagull will be a mile away by the time Albert gets back with the toilet paper."

Just so! It's hard to know where a humorous story will go once it's uttered. It's also often impossible to know where a story comes from. An anecdote about a mysterious distant voice illustrates this.

2. Ernest and Herbert were religious doubters, but they had a little bit of faith. They agreed that the one who died first would make every effort to communicate with the other. Herbert was the first to "depart." For many months, Ernest kept alert, hoping to hear from him. Finally, one night he awoke from a deep sleep and heard a familiar voice calling, "Ernest! Ernest!"

"Herbert!" cried Ernest. "You've done it! I heard you! Tell me, what's it like?"

"Well," said Herbert, "it's not bad. I'm in a very comfortable, calm, dark place. After enjoying sleep, I come out and eat in beautiful green meadows. Then I have a little sex and go back into my dark comfort. After a lovely sleep, again I feel hungry, so I have some more lovely green food to eat, and then a little sex, and then back again to sleep."

"Golly," said Ernest, "so that's what Heaven is like!"

"Heaven?" said Herbert. "Who said I was in Heaven? I'm a rabbit in Altoona, Pa."

Just as Ernest didn't know where the voice came from, we often don't know where funny stories originate. As that wonderful humorist and linguist Leo Rosten says in his *Hooray for Yiddish!*—which is full of funny stories old and new—classic jokes "have an independent life, and immortal viability. . . . Before you growl 'I read that one before!' let me say 'So what?' Do you stop a pianist who is playing Chopin because you heard that piece before?''

Eric W. Johnson

1.

Sexuality, Sex, Reproduction, and Sex Education

This chapter comes first because all of us are sexually conceived, and we all are, to a greater or lesser extent, sexual beings right on through the last chapter, "Old Age." You will find nothing "off-color" here—but don't worry; there's a lot of that in Chapter 4, "Language."

So, where shall we start on sex? Let's have a safe one: learning about reproduction.

3. When a precocious nine-year-old girl was asked by her teacher to write an essay on "Where My Family Came From," she decided to undertake a bit of research. So, before supper she sat at the table where she often did her homework and asked her mother some questions.

"Mom, where did I come from?"

Her mother, being a bit old-fashioned, found herself saying, "Well, the stork brought you, dear."

"Where did *you* come from, then?"

"Uh, the stork brought me, too."

"Okay, then where did Granny come from?"

"The stork brought her, too, dear."

"Okay, thanks, Mom," said the girl, who settled

down to writing her homework. After about five minutes the mother happened to walk by her daughter and read the first sentence of the essay: "For three generations there have been no natural births in our family."

Enlightened families should not give their young daughters such problems. It's amazing, though, how many people there are who, for reasons best known to them, oppose sex education in schools.

4. A community was rocked by a great debate: Should sex education be taught in the third grade? A PTA meeting was called, and there was lively discussion of all the issues. During the debate, one parent stood up and said, very earnestly, "I'm not opposed to sex education. We need it. But eight is much too young to be calling things by their right names!"

Well, I'm generally in favor of using "right names." Euphemisms can get you into trouble.

5. A mother carefully explained to her young daughter how children were created. She used the expression "carrying a child" instead of "pregnant," but the girl seemed satisfied.

Sometime later, a terrible fire broke out in the neighborhood, and the girl stood by watching. Here's how she described the scene to her parents: "There was this big fire, and a fireman ran into the house, and when he came out, he was pregnant."

"Carrying a baby" is a pleasant-enough phrase. But, according to my pregnant friends' reports over the years, the condition calls for other comments.

6. One of the questions pregnant women get asked most often is, "When are you going to have your baby?" Different professional people comment on the condition in other ways, however. For example:

> *Pilots:* "I see you have one in the hangar."
> *Photo lab workers;* "Still have one in the developer, I see."
> *Librarians:* "Aren't you overdue?"

Back again to euphemisms, pregnancy, and the troubles these things can cause logical young observers of prenatal progress:

7. A boy and his father had gone over the facts of life, which was necessary because Mother was pregnant. "You see, son, you could say that I've given your mother a new baby." The boy was impressed.

Several months went by, and then the boy seemed troubled. Finally, he went to his father and said, "Dad, you know that baby you gave Mommy? Well, she's eaten it."

Where do babies go after being "given" is one question. Another is, where do they come from?

8. A young girl was very much interested in the progress of her mother's pregnancy. Finally, the day of birth drew near and the girl overheard arrangements being made for her mother to go to the hospital. She looked at her mother with great puzzlement and said, "Mom, I don't understand. If they're going to deliver the baby, why do you have to go to the hospital?"

We haven't yet seen all available examples of what children don't know about sex, reproduction, and other "related" questions.

9. Children's misconceptions about marriage, pregnancy, and childbirth:
- To pet dog: "I'd like to marry you, Prince, but you're not allowed to marry anyone in your own family."
- "All I want to know is: Who's the opposite sex, her or me?"
- "If mothers can give birth to boys, why do we need fathers?"
- "The stork only brings the parts. The doctor puts them together."
- "Last year my mother came down with a baby. Now my aunt's got it."

And, of course, having babies means that parents can "come down with" serious financial consequences.

10. A man who was not very well paid, yet who had several children, learned a distressing piece of news from his wife. The next morning he called his insurance company to ask a weighty question, to which the reply was, "No, Mr. Korman, your wife's pregnancy is not covered by your accident insurance."

This leads to some rather naive confusion about educational basics—reading, writing, and arithmetic—and reproduction.

11. Mother and father rabbit were talking about the children after they had been put to bed. "Why was Junior so happy this evening?" asked father rabbit.

"Well," explained mother rabbit, "he had a marvelous time at school. He learned to multiply."

12. A second grader came home from school and said to her mother, "Mom, guess what? We learned how to make babies today."

The mother, more than a little surprised, tried to keep her cool. "That's interesting," she said. "How do you make babies?"

"It's simple," replied the girl. "You just change *y* to *i* and add *es*."

Sex education is certainly needed, but many people are still rather nervous about it, especially parents.

13. A unit in sex education was about to begin, and each student had to bring in a permission slip in order to take it. A boy handed in his slip and explained to the teacher, "My mom says I can take the course as long as there's no homework."

Now let's get into the world of sexuality at a somewhat more "sophisticated" level.

14. A young man who traveled a good deal liked to collect exotic pieces of art. He displayed one of his treasures, an ancient fertility symbol, on the fireplace mantel. One evening he brought an attractive young woman back to his apartment. "Excuse me for just a moment," he said. "I want to get into something a bit more comfortable."

While he was gone, the woman looked around the living room and suddenly stopped in front of the statuette on the mantel. When the man came back, she asked him what it was.

"Oh," said he, a little embarrassed, "that's called a phallus."

"Thanks," she replied. "I'd hate to tell you what it *looks* like."

Of course, art can be sexy and, at the same time, very beautiful, as viewers of nude paintings know. But you may not realize *all* the difficulties artists can get into.

15. The famous painter Maxfield Parrish (1870–1966), who illustrated *The Arabian Nights* and painted that remarkable fresco in the King Cole Bar at the St. Regis Hotel in New York, sometimes had difficulty getting down to work, even though one of his specialties was painting voluptuous nudes.

Well, one morning a beautiful young model arrived at his studio to pose. Parrish said, "I don't feel like working right now. Let's have a cup of coffee."

Parrish got the coffee, and they sat down. At that moment, the studio door-telephone buzzer rang. Parrish answered it and then quickly put his hand over the receiver.

"Young lady," he cried, "for God's sake take off your clothes. My wife is coming to check up on me."

And it's not only artists who can get into trouble with their spouses, or at least find themselves in embarrassing situations. The key question is: Is honesty the best policy?

16. A few years ago, the chairman of the board of a well-known private school was invited to talk to the student body. "Well, all right," said the chairman. "What subject would you like me to talk about?"

The headmaster replied, "It would be very helpful if you'd give them a talk about *sex*."

After a little hesitation, the chairman accepted. But when he got home, he didn't quite dare tell his wife the subject he was given, so he told a white lie: "I was asked to talk on *sailing*." His wife seemed puzzled, but the conversation moved on to other things.

A few days later, a school parent remarked to the chairman's wife, "Your husband made a wonderful talk to the student body."

"I'm amazed," said the wife. "He's only done it three times. The first time he got sick to his stomach. The second time his hat blew off. And the third time his foot got caught in the sheet."

This difficulty is quite different from that of two parents who were very much worried by the way modern youth behave.

17. Karen, the teenage daughter, had been out on a date, and she didn't get back home until 3 A.M., when her mother sneaked downstairs to check on her. The mother and father were discussing the matter the next morning.

Mother: I'm really worried about Karen.

Father: Why?

Mother: Well, you never woke up, but I can tell you she didn't get in till 3 A.M.

Father: That's pretty late. But she's a good girl, and kids do stay out late these days.

Mother: Yes, but that's not all. I noticed that when she came in she was carrying a Gideon Bible!

The worlds of the phallus collector, the painter of nudes, and the modern teenager are far removed—it is said, but who knows?—from those of the stereotypical "maiden ladies," or spinsters, as they are called in England. Here's a story about monogamy taken to extremes.

18. A rather prim maiden lady, after working at a city job for over thirty years, decided to resign, take her savings, and go to the country and start a poultry farm. She purchased a country cottage with enough land to build chicken coops. When they were done she went into the village to place her order for the poultry. "I want sixty hens," she said to the salesperson, "and sixty roosters."

Even scientists have their ideas of what's proper, as this true story (told to me by a friend) shows.

19. A researcher studying the methods of reproduction of very minute creatures was looking intensely into the microscope. Suddenly she exclaimed, "Wow! How can they do *that* in broad daylight?"

But most sexual activity, I believe, happens after dark. At least this is the case in the feline world. And if this story seems to be an insult to teachers, blame it on George Bernard Shaw (1856–1950), who greatly enjoyed insulting people. It is Shaw who is paraphrased at the end of this story.

20. A family owned a tomcat, of whom it was normally quite fond. Quite often, however, the cat would get out at night and go around the neighborhood howling and screeching and meowing so loudly that people would complain. So the family took the tom to a vet and had him fixed.

A few nights later, though, the cat was out again, and this time he was making even more noise than usual. Not only that, but a lot of other cats were howling and yelling, too. The father of the house went out to see what was going on. He caught the cat's attention and asked, "What are you doing? You're supposed to be over all this."

"Oh," replied the cat, "He who can, *does*; he who cannot, *teaches*." [An alternative, more "contemporary" reply: "Well, now I'm serving as a consultant."]

Even popes have personal troubles with people and sexuality—and not just in the confessional.

21. Pope John XXIII (1881–1963; pope, 1958–1963) told of a particular difficulty he would commonly have when he was the Vatican's diplomatic envoy to France. "The problem with these receptions," he told a friend, "is that if a woman arrives wearing a gown that is cut daringly low, everybody gazes not at the lady but at me, to see if I'm looking at the lady."

22. Remember this now-outdated definition of a psychiatrist? "The one who, when a beautiful woman enters the room, looks at everyone else." I've found this definition still fits other classes of people, though. I was once with a group that was hiking through the White Mountains of New Hampshire. We were eating sandwiches by the side of a trail when an attractive—

and topless—young woman walked by and sat quite conspicuously on a bluff above us. We all looked at her except for the ministers, of whom there were several among us. They attended strictly to their sandwiches.

And speaking of psychiatrists (some of my best friends are, and to them I apologize), how about this?

23. A psychiatrist was asked whether he talked with his wife after sexual intercourse.

The psychiatrist replied, "Only if there's a telephone."

But let's move from psychiatrists to psychologists. A friend of mine reported that the following happened at the University of Chicago.

24. The famous psychologist Bruno Bettelheim (1903–1990), author of *Love Is Not Enough* and *The Uses of Enchantment*, taught for many years at the University of Chicago. In one of his courses, he was annoyed by a young woman student who was knitting during his lectures. Finally, he stopped in mid-lecture and said to the student, "Young woman, do you know what you are really doing when you knit like that? You're masturbating."

"Well, professor," replied the student, "I'll do it my way, you do it your way."

Let's face it, no matter how it is done, masturbation is a subject many people, unless they are Bruno Bettelheim, just don't like to talk about. And yet people *need* to talk about it; and in my sex education classes, I encourage my students to do so. My rule is this: Just be sure they know the facts, so they can make their *own* decisions. Sometimes, though, it's easier for them to write about it than talk.

25. An eighth-grade boy to whom I taught sex education a number of years ago chose to write a short paper on the subject of masturbation. His final paragraph read: "I really don't see what's wrong with masturbation. It's always available. It doesn't cost anything. You don't get anybody pregnant. You don't catch any diseases. And you meet a better class of people."

A subject that interests more and more people these days is sexuality and aging—and remember, sexuality and pleasure consist of more than just sexual intercourse. Here's another true story.

26. A younger man, Roger, was a faithful visitor of an 82-year-old woman, Alicia, in a nursing home. They knew each other well and enjoyed each other's company. Alicia could not walk and was confined to her bed or a wheelchair. One evening she was in her wheelchair and looked up at Roger: "Would you mind if I asked you to scratch my back?"

"Of course not," replied Roger. So Alicia leaned forward and loosened her garments a little. Roger reached around and gently scratched her, and obviously it felt good.

"Do you know, Roger," she said, "I think the back is the least embarrassing part of the human body."

Roger went on gently scratching, and then Alicia added, with a bit of a twinkle, ". . . although it leads to a thing or two."

So much for elderly women. What about priests? Are they alone immune to sexual desire?

27. A young priest was troubled by the fact that he was very much attracted by young women. He felt this was sinful, so he went to an older colleague, a 76-year-old priest. "Father," he asked after explaining his problem, "at what age do you get over this trouble?"

The older priest replied, "Three days after you're dead."

The next story deals with another problem of sex and the elderly. Fortunately—and this is true of many older people I know—the oldster in this story kept his sense of humor.

28. A very conservative doctor was consulted by an older man who wasn't feeling very well. After a thorough medical checkup, the doctor said, "Mr. Kramer, I can't find anything specifically wrong with you. I have only one suggestion—that you—eh, eh—give up some of your love life."

There was a long pause, and then Mr. Kramer said, "O.K., Doc. But which half should I give up: thinking about it or talking about it?"

Let's move to the United Kingdom and read about the higher British orders. This story's about a lady who knew how to defend her right *not* to be considered a "sex object."

29. Some time ago, after an elaborate service at St. Paul's Cathedral in London, where servants of the empire were invested into the Knights of the Grand Cross of the Order of the British Empire, the Air Chief Marshal attended a civic luncheon given by the Lord Mayor of London. He found himself seated next to the Lady Mayoress, a very amply proportioned woman who was wearing her Mayoral chain and a red rose in her bosom.

The Air Chief Marshal, still wearing his robes and the gold chain of the Order, looked at the Mayoress's rose thoughtfully and, as he sat down next to her, said with a smile, "Lady Mayoress, if I were to pluck your rose, would you blush?"

"Marshal," replied the lady without hesitation, "and if I were to pull your chain, would you flush?"

Now we switch to the great Philadelphia Zoo. What are the attitudes about sex there?

30. A visitor to the Philadelphia Zoo asked a keeper, "Is that a male or a female hippopotamus?"

The keeper replied, "That, madam, is something that should be of interest only to another hippopotamus."

And so we have the hippo-human gap. How about the generation gap? This story illustrates how it can befuddle even enlightened women.

31. A young married woman and an old married woman happened to be riding together on the train from Boston to New York. As sometimes happens with strangers in such an environment, they began to discuss highly personal matters. As they were passing through Hartford, the younger woman spoke up thoughtfully, "Tell me, do you and your husband have mutual orgasm?"

"No," replied the older lady, "I think we have State Farm."

And here's another story about a generation gap. It took place back in the sixties.

32. Two hippies came before a justice of the peace to be married. Looking at their clothes and hair, the justice couldn't tell which was male and which female. So he looked at one and asked, "Are you the one with the menstrual cycle?" The hippie replied, "No, man, I got a Honda."

A few pages ago, I told you about a cat who quoted George Bernard Shaw. Here's a story about the man himself.

33. George Bernard Shaw (1856–1950), the great Irish-born playwright and critic, was sitting at dinner beside a very attractive woman. Shaw asked her, "Madame, would you go to bed with me for £5000?"

The woman looked astonished and hemmed and hawed a bit.

Shaw then asked, "Well, how about for £50,000?"

The woman still could not answer.

"Well, look," said Shaw, "would you go to bed with me for £12?"

"Mr. Shaw!" the woman exclaimed, "what do you think I am?"

Shaw replied, "We've already established that, Madame. We're just negotiating the price."

These days we hear a good deal about "safe sex" and condoms. That's not all condoms are good for, though.

34. An attractive young woman, all dressed up for dinner, was caught in a sudden rainstorm. Drenched, she needed a cigarette. As an equally attractive friend watched, she reached into her bra and pulled out a small rubber thing, opened it, and took out a perfectly dry cigarette. It was in a condom.

Her friend said, "That's a good idea! I'll have to try it."

So the next day the friend went to a drugstore and said, "A package of condoms, please."

"What size?" asked the salesperson.

"I guess it should be big enough for a Camel."

One of the biggest problems we have is keeping sex in perspective with the rest of life. Here's one about a boy who didn't have that problem:

35. The following letter was received by the Library of Congress from a schoolboy:

Dear Sirs:

Can you give me the name of a good book on aeronautics and also one on sane sex life. I am more interested in aeronautics.

The next story also shows a good sense of proportion about life. It happened in one of my own sex education classes at Germantown Friends School.

36. My eighth-graders were discussing the difference between men and women. There were a good many statements about how men tend to be bolder, stronger, louder, and more decisive than women, and a good deal of disagreement, like, "Yeah, but I know a woman who's a lot stronger and bolder than her husband," and so forth. Very few generalizations about "all" men or "all" women seemed supportable. Then the discussion went like this:

Teacher: Well, is there anything that's different between *all* men and *all* women?

Girl: Yes, men have penises; women don't. Women have vaginas; men don't. [A general nodding of heads and a few giggles]

Teacher: Any comments about that?

Boy: Sure. The more times a man can have sexual intercourse—*copulate*, do you call it?—the more of a man he is.

Teacher [after quite a few murmurs of protest, and a couple of "Yeah!"s]: O.K. Wait a minute. There may be more to being a "real man," as they say, than how many times you copulate over a period of time. What about that?

Boy: Well, I remember in kindergarten and first and second grades, we had guinea pigs in the homeroom, and boy could they copulate!

Girl: Yeah, and not only guinea pigs, but mice and hamsters, and rabbits. They were always doing it.

Teacher: So?

Another boy: So, if you try to prove yourself a real man by the number of times you copulate, you *don't* prove you're a real man. You prove that you're a real guinea pig, mouse, or hamster. Or rabbit. No thanks!

I'll finish this chapter on sexuality with the best tongue-in-cheek example of putting sex in perspective that I have ever read. It concerns that once-notorious book, banned from many libraries and forbidden to children and to adolescents, *Lady Chatterley's Lover*, by D. H. Lawrence (1885–1930). Parts of the book were sexually very explicit—so much so that only an expurgated edition could be published in England in 1928, and it took the French to publish a full edition in Paris, in 1929.

37. Here is a review of *Lady Chatterley's Lover*, printed, appropriately enough, in *Field and Stream*, November 1959:

"Although written many years ago, *Lady Chatterley's Lover* has just been reissued by Grove Press, and this fictional account of the day-by-day life of an English gamekeeper is still of considerable interest to outdoor-minded readers, as it contains many passages on pheasant raising, the apprehending of poachers, ways to control vermin, and other chores and duties of the professional gamekeeper. Unfortunately one is obliged to wade through many pages of extraneous materials in order to discover and savor these sidelights on the management of a Midlands shooting estate, and in this reviewer's opinion this book cannot take the place of J. R. Miller's *Practical Gamekeeping*."

2.

Children and Adolescents— with Compliments to Both

All of us are, or have been, children, and will be, are, or have been adolescents—people on the way to becoming adults. Who was it who said, "Scratch an adult and you'll find a child"? So scratch your way through this chapter and perhaps you'll find yourself between the lines—or on them.

We'll begin on an optimistic yet realistic note.

38. A *Foolproof Recipe for Preserving Children
(Receta Infalible para Conservar Ninos)*

A South American cookbook, helping to prove that there's something universal about children, outdoors, and joy, gives this recipe: "Take one large grassy field, one half dozen children, two or three small dogs, a pinch of brook, and some pebbles. Mix the children and the dogs well together, stirring constantly. Pour the brook over the pebbles. Sprinkle the field with flowers. Spread a deep blue sky over all and bake in a hot sun. When done remove and set away to soak in a bathtub."

Sounds nice, doesn't it? However, as the next several stories show, there's an element of vigor, and even violence, in children that makes them a challenge.

39. A twelve-year-old boy, the son of a British military attaché, was asked by his grandmother what he wanted to be. He replied, very thoughtfully: "Well, maybe a policeman. . . . No, not that. . . . Maybe a tank driver. . . . No, not that. . . . Oh, I know, a terrorist."

40. Nine-year-old Aaron came home from the playground with a bloody nose, black eye, and torn clothing. It was obvious he'd been in a bad fight and lost. While his father was patching him up, he asked his son what happened.

"Well, Dad," said Aaron, "I challenged Larry to a duel. And, you know, I gave him his choice of weapons."

"Uh-huh," said the father, "that seems fair."

"I know, but I never thought he'd choose his sister!"

41. Ozzie came home from school with a black eye and cut lips. His mother sighed deeply, "Oh, Ozzie, you've been in another fight."

"But, Mom," sniffled Ozzie, "I was just keeping a little boy from being beaten up by a bigger boy."

"Well," said Mom, "that was brave. Who was the little boy?"

"Me, Mommy."

42. A small girl, her young brother, and the baby were together in the living room. The babysitter was out in the kitchen getting some milk and cookies when she heard the baby yelping. She came quickly into the living room and saw the boy pinching the baby.

"Willy," shouted the babysitter, "why are you pinching the baby?"

"We're playing automobile," said his sister, "and the baby is the horn."

A babysitter with three youngsters to care for has problems, yes, but:

43. According to one parental couple I know, nothing is harder than putting on a birthday party for small kids, especially when pony rides are included. The father told me that as a result of such a party he had discovered a *new* Theory of Relativity. You know, possibly, that Einstein's theory is $E = mc^2$, where $E =$ energy, and $m =$ mass. What c equals I'm never quite sure, but it has something to do with time and motion—squared!—and that's a lot of time and motion. The new *Birthday Theory of Relativity* (BTR) is: "The faster the kids move the slower time goes for the adults responsible—squared!"

How about the *real* experts on childhood? Can *they* deal with all these things complacently and competently?

44. Angelo Patri (1877–1965), a famous Italian-born American expert on child behavior, one day observed three children walking on a newly laid cement sidewalk. He grew very angry and was about to rush out of the house and chase them off when his wife said, "But, Angelo, you *love* children."

"Yes," said Patri, as he left the house, "I love them in the abstract, but not in the concrete."

One of the wonderful things about children is that they are ready to leap right in and be helpful even though they may not fully understand what's involved. One might even say that they are overconfident.

45. A salesman telephoned a household, and a four-year-old boy answered. The conversation went thus:

Salesman: May I speak to your mother?

Boy: She's not here.

Salesman: Well, is anyone else there?

Boy: My sister.

Salesman: O.K., fine. May I speak to her?

Boy: I guess so.

At this point there was a very long silence on the phone. Then:

Boy: Hello?

Salesman: It's you. I thought you were going to call your sister.

Boy: I did. The trouble is, I can't get her out of the playpen.

Here's another story of overconfidence.

46. A girl, who was not quite four years old, was alone in the house when the phone rang. She answered it and was told that Mr. Brown was calling. "I'm sorry, no one is here. Can I take a message?" After a pause, Mr. Brown heard, "O.K., I'm ready. Who is this did you say?"

"Mr. Brown."

"How do you spell Brown?"

"B-r-o-w-n."

A long pause, and then, "How do you make a B?"

Another trait young children have is their confident knowledge of obvious truths that aren't true.

47. At the supper table, one child asked, "Why is cream so much more expensive than milk?"

"It's obvious," replied another. "It's harder for the cow to sit on the little bottle."

48. During a dinner party, the hosts' two little children entered the dining room totally nude and walked slowly around the table. The parents were so embarrassed that they pretended nothing was happening and kept the conversation going. The guests cooperated and also continued as if nothing extraordinary was happening.

After going all the way around the room, the children left, and there was a moment of silence at the table, during which one child was heard to say, "You see, it *is* vanishing cream!"

Children as we have seen, tend to take things too literally and draw erroneous conclusions.

49. Six-year-old Gilbert, who watched a good many TV ads, was asked by his pediatrician, just to make conversation, "Gil, if you found a couple of dollars and had to spend them, what would you buy?"

"A box of Tampax," he replied without hesitation.

"Tampax?" said the doctor. "What would you do with that?"

"Well," said Gil, "I don't know exactly know, but it's sure worth two dollars. Why with Tampax, it says on TV, you can go swimming, go horseback riding, and also go skating, any time you want to."

Here's another story about a precocious child. Pediatricians, watch out!

50. Three-and-a-half-year-old Ronnie Gilson was taken by his mother to a pediatrician for a physical checkup. When they entered the office, the dialogue went like this:

Pediatrician: Good morning, Ronnie. Good morning, Mrs. Gilson.

The Gilsons: Good morning, Doctor.

Pediatrician (after asking Ronnie to be seated and hoping to make him feel at ease): Ronnie, I want to ask you a few questions.

Ronnie: O.K., Doc.

Pediatrician (touching Ronnie's nose): Is this your nose?

Ronnie: Yes.

Pediatrician (touching Ronnie's mouth): Is this your mouth?

Ronnie: Yep.

Pediatrician (wanting to see whether Ronnie really knew what he was answering, and touching the boy's ear): And is this is one of your eyes?

Ronnie (turning to his mother): Mom, I think we'd better see another doctor.

Children are also quite practical and don't always bother with the higher meaning of things like holidays.

51. A bunch of young kids in a large family were enjoying Easter eggs and chocolate rabbits. One, remembering experiences of trick-or-treating, remarked, "Easter tastes better than Halloween, and you don't have to ring a lot of doorbells."

Now let's shift upwards in age and consider some stories about adolescents, who may act like kids one day and adults the next. It can be a difficult time.

52. A young teenager said to her mother, "I feel so nervous."

Her mother: "What do you mean, 'nervous'?"

"Well," said the girl, "I feel in a hurry all over, but I can't get started."

53. There is a widespread tendency among adolescents to feel that they are more grown up than they are, that they should be given privileges their parents or teachers don't think they are ready for. A ninth-grade girl in Newark, N.J., wrote this on the subject: "The more I think about it, the more I think the age of twenty-five should be lowered to eighteen."

A sense of perspective about life is something that older people have (see the final chapter) but not adolescents. Consider this:

54. A young girl was writing to her friend, listing the gifts she had received upon her graduation from junior high school. She wrote, ". . . and Grandma gave me a diary. It is a nice diary, but it's awfully late to start on a diary now. Everything has happened."

But other adolescents, if you can consider age eighteen still a part of adolescence, are eagerly looking for wisdom and perspective.

55. Some older friends were dining at a restaurant, and one said how interesting it would be if you could turn back the clock and live your life over again.

"Well, you know what I would like?" said another diner. "I'd like to be eighteen years old but to know what I know now."

At this point the counter waitress, who had been clearing the table, stopped and said, "I'm eighteen. What is it you know?"

What about mere adolescents getting married? It sometimes happens.

56. A sixteen-year-old boy and a fifteen-year-old girl wanted to get married. Both sets of parents objected strenuously, but the young lovers were absolutely insistent. They loved each other and they wanted to get married—and in a church. "If you won't let us," the girl said to her parents, "we'll just run away and get married."

So it was agreed—a small ceremony in the church, attended only by the young couple and the four parents. The minister was performing the ceremony; the young couple repeating his words after him.

Minister: With all my wordly goods I thee endow.

Boy: With all my wordly goods I thee endow.

Boy's mother (whispering to his father): There goes his bicycle.

A classic objection to adolescent behavior: They hog the telephone.

57. A teenage girl had been talking on the phone for about half an hour, and then she hung up.

"Gee," said her father, "that was short. You usually talk for two hours. What happened?"

"Wrong number," replied the girl.

Parents must be careful not to be too critical of their teenagers lest they get totally discouraged. Remember: "Courage is the memory of past successes." The following story has a deep element of sadness in it.

58. Two adolescent girls were relaxing together on a sofa, conversing, bringing up their deepest feelings about life. When the talk turned to families, one friend turned to the other and said, "You know? The trouble with me is, I'm the sort of person my mother doesn't want me to associate with."

But some adolescents know how to appeal to our basic love for them and to get us to look on their positive sides.

59. An adolescent who felt she was getting criticized too much at home and school became tired of defending herself all the time. So she made up a large button and pinned it to her blouse: "Please be patient. God has not finished with me yet."

Certainly one of the ways that children, adolescents, and adults can get along better is to consider how their actions affect others. Perhaps a good way to close this chapter is with a story that illustrates consideration of others—or at least of *some* others!

60. In the crowded and hot Nieman-Marcus department store in Dallas, two small children, Sally and her younger brother Jimmy, were eating ice cream cones and riding up and down the escalators. While going up an escalator, their ice cream cones melting and dripping, Sally was behind Jimmy, and Jimmy was crowded against the back of a woman wearing an expensive, mink stole. Sally was horrified. ''Watch out, Jimmy,'' she said, ''you're getting fur all over your ice cream!''

3.

Family Life, Marriage, and Relationships

Families, in one way or dozens, are a part of our lives, as are marriage and children, our own or those of others, for better or for worse—or both. To wit:

"Keep your eyes wide open before marriage, half shut afterward."—Benjamin Franklin (1706–1790)

"He that hath wife and children hath given hostages to fortune; for they are impediments to great enterprises, either of virtue or mischief."—Francis Bacon (1561–1626)

"Most of the persons whom I see in my own house I see across a gulf."—Ralph Waldo Emerson (1803–1882)

"God gives us relatives; thank God, we can choose our friends."—Addison Mizner (1872–1933)

But humor can fix all—well, *some*—of this.

Obviously, one of the main tasks of parents of families is bringing up children—better for them to be soundly brought up than for the parents to fit this definition: "*Parent*—Something so simple even a child can operate it." Obedience is important.

61. A mother firefly was taking her children for a walk near dusk, and they came to a dark woods. "All right, kids," she ordered, "line up, and whatever happens, don't shine your light. There are owls in the forest and they might fly down and eat you!"

The small fireflies did as they were told, with the youngest firefly at the end of the line. As they were moving carefully along, suddenly the mother saw a light far back.

"Stop!" she whispered. "Who lit the light back there?"

"I did," admitted the youngster.

"You heard what I told you," scolded the mother. "Why did you disobey?"

"Well," said the little one, "when you gotta glow, you gotta glow."

Of course, we should remember what the firefly said when it backed into the lawnmower: "De-lighted, no end."

Sometimes children *do* obey . . . but with unexpected results.

62. The father of the family was ordered to follow a strict diet, which forced the whole family to change its eating habits: no red meat, no fancy foods, mostly fish and vegetables. This was a new experience for Alex, the youngest boy.

One evening the mother served fish and cauliflower for supper. They all started gravely to eat, until the boy, chewing on his fish, found a bone. He pulled it out of his mouth and asked, "Mom, what do I do with this?"

"Put it where you're sure you won't eat it," said his mother. So the boy carefully stuck it into his cauliflower.

It's good to know that, basically, children love their parents—even very famous children, as they remember it later.

63. James McNeill Whistler (1834–1903) was asked by a Boston dowager why he was born in Lowell, Massachusetts. He replied, "Because I wanted to be near my mother." [*Note:* Whistler's famous portrait of his mother (1872), "Arrangement in Gray and Black," hangs in the Louvre.]

It couldn't have been baby Whistler about whom the following comment was made.

64. Some wise guy said: "I saw a baby playing in the playpen. I noticed it had its mother's eyes, its mother's nose, and its mother's mouth—which, if you ask me, left its mother with a pretty blank expression."

It's nice, of course, to have children concerned for the well-being of their parents.

65. Lance, age four, was very cross at the supper table.

"The trouble with you is," said his mother, "you didn't take a nap this afternoon."

Lance looked at his mother directly and said, "Yes, and what's *your* trouble?"

So, what theories can we expound for bringing up children?

66. Lord Rochester, John Wilmot (1647–1680), said to a group, "When I was young, I had six theories on how to bring up children."

"And, pray, what are your theories?" asked someone.

"There is no use in asking," replied Rochester. "Now I have six children and no theories."

Children, theories or no theories, surely realize that they are difficult, and they often admit it—with a twist.

67. The parents of a teenager got very tired of their daughter's bad attitude. "The trouble with you, Julie," said her mother, "is that all you do is grumble and complain."

"That's not so—it's not even fair," snarled Julie. "I also gripe, crab, bellyache, carp, and grouse."

And here's a younger child who was also realistic about herself.

68. The teacher explained the meaning of the word *responsibility* to his second-grade class. Then, to reinforce the lesson, he asked the children to tell about their responsibilities at home. "My responsibility," said one particularly strenuous little girl, "is to get out and stay out."

Perhaps it was that same little second grader who inspired this comment.

69. A couple of friends were discussing the behavior of a child they couldn't stand. "It's a pity," one said, "birth control can't be made retroactive."

The child in the next story wouldn't go so far as to advocate such a use of birth control, but she had ideas about birth—and great faith in her mother.

70. A small girl's father asked her what she would most like for Christmas. The girl, knowing that her mother was expecting, replied, "A baby brother." To everyone's delight, the mother came back from the hospital on Christmas Eve with a baby boy in her arms.

Some time later, the father said to his daughter, "And *next* Christmas what would you like?"

"Well," said the girl, after some thought, "if it wouldn't be too uncomfortable for Mom, I'd like a pony."

I guess all of us are selfish, but children are probably more so than adults, despite what Jesus of Nazareth said about not getting into heaven unless you become like a little child.

71. The mother of a small girl was concerned about her child's selfish behavior and gave her something of a lecture, stressing that we are put in this world to help others.

Her daughter seemed much impressed and sat silently, thinking and scratching her head. At last she looked up and said, "Mommy?"

"Yes, dear?" replied her mother.

"What I want to know is, what are the *others* for?"

Or, as another child put it when asked to repeat the Golden Rule, "Do unto others before they do unto you."
Yes, children *can* be selfish, but maybe that's healthy.

72. The family was ordering hamburgers in a restaurant.

Waitress: Now, how will you have your hamburger?
Father: Rare.
Mother: Medium.
Child: Large.

73. Mother, father, and small son were out to dinner. The waitress took the parents' orders and then turned to the boy. "What will you have?" she asked.

"I'd like a hot dog, and—" the boy began.

"No, no," the mother interrupted, "no hot dogs. He'll have beef, potatoes, milk. . . ."

But the waitress ignored the mother and asked the boy, "Ketchup or mustard on the hot dog?"

"Ketchup," replied the boy, smiling, "and a Coke."

The waitress turned away and started for the kitchen saying, "Coming up!"

The parents were dumbfounded. Then the kid said to them, "Know what? She thinks I'm real."

Children can have an exaggerated idea of their own powers.

74. A young girl's father had been in the hospital for a serious operation, and for several days he could not receive visitors. Still in pretty bad shape, he was finally allowed a visit from his family. His young daughter was baffled by her father's condition. "But, Dad, you look awful! Didn't you get my get-well card?"

They can also give a loving put-down.

75. "Well, Son," said the father, "whatever else you can say about me, I'm a self-made man."

"That's what I like about you, Pop," replied the son. "You are always willing to take the blame for everything."

What parents need to take from their children is recognized quite widely.

76. A woman was applying for the renewal of her driver's license. She was asked by the inspector, "Have you ever been adjudged insane or feeble-minded?" He paused and smiled, adding, "That is, by anyone other than your own children?"

77. Two children were sitting on the front porch talking about families. One asked the other, "Do you believe in Planned Parenthood?"

"I sure do," was the reply. "I wish I could have planned mine."

78. A similar conversation between two somewhat older kids, perhaps the same ones, went as follows: "When you grow up, do you want to have children?" "Sure, I do, but I wouldn't want to be a—, a—, you know, a parent."

However, parents do have their importance, a fact that was recognized by the modern-age kid in this story.

79. In a family where there were four small children, the father had gone off to work. The mother was sick in bed. The telephone rang and a seven-year-old answered it. "Hello?"

"Yes?"

After a pause: "I'm sorry. Our computer is down. Please call back tomorrow."

One of the trying issues in family life is order and cleanliness. If you don't believe it, read on.

80. A small boy came running downstairs, shouting, "Mom! Mom! I cleaned my room without being told!"

"Well," said his mother, "that's wonderful! Thank you very much. It will save me a lot of trouble, and it shows you're growing up."

"Yeah, but, Mom," said the boy, "don't jump to conclusions."

"I don't understand, dear," said his mother. "Conclusions?"

"Yeah, Mom," said the boy. "This isn't going to become a habit."

81. An adolescent who felt she had the right to do anything she pleased with her own room, and yet who was very conscious of the importance of making a better world, was called downstairs by her parents.

"Yeah, Mom 'n' Dad, what is it now?" she asked.

"It's your room," replied her parents.

"I know it's *my* room," she replied, "and I have a right to keep things the way I want to."

"But," said her mother, "when anyone opens the door, things spill out into the hall, and the air coming out under the door doesn't smell very good."

"Well, so what are you going to do about it? I'm pretty busy with my work," said the girl.

Her father replied, "We're going to give you a choice. Either clean up your room or file an environmental impact statement."

82. Mother had just finished waxing the floors when she heard her young son opening the front door. She shouted, "Be careful on that floor, Jimmy; it's just been waxed."

Jimmy, walking right in, replied, "Don't worry, Mom, I'm wearing my cleats."

83. It was a muddy day, and little Julius had been playing outside. Around lunchtime he opened the door and came right into the kitchen. His mother said angrily, "Julius, look at all the dirt you've tracked in."

Julius retorted, "Yeah, I suppose so, Mom, but I notice you never mention the dirt I track out."

The following story comes from Mary S. Calderone, a coauthor of mine, a leading sex educator, and a fellow Quaker. The protagonist is her great-granddaughter.

84. Three-year-old Arianna was playing in the kitchen where her mother was working. She was getting a bit in the way, and mother said, "Please go upstairs and help Dad with the work he is doing."

Arianna replied, "I can't. I'm thinking."

A little later, Arianna was still in the way, and her mother said somewhat impatiently, "Now, Arianna, you've just got to go upstairs and help Dad."

Arianna sighed, got up, went to the stairs, and started to climb, slowly. As she went she was heard to remark to herself, perhaps intending to be overheard,

"They just don't give you any chance to think around here."

Parents do get desperate. What can they possibly do to control their kids?

85. Two rebellious teenagers were with their mother at Mesa Verde National Park in Colorado. There were signs that made it very clear that footwear was required in the park. However, the youngsters argued that they had tough feet, that the signs were not important, and "who cares anyway?" It became quite a shouting match.

Finally, in desperation the mother said, "O.K., do what you want, *but don't call me Mother!*"

86. The parents of a difficult boy were discussing what to give him for a birthday present. The mother said, "Let's buy him a bicycle."

"Well," said the father, "maybe—but do you think it will improve his behavior?"

"Probably not," said the mother, "but it will spread it over a wider area."

87. The minister of a well-attended, strong, and enthusiastic church often showed himself ready and able to deal with any situation that might come up. One Sunday, just as the minister was reaching the climax of his sermon, his own young son entered the church, ran to the center aisle, started making loud beeps and brrrmms like a car without a muffler, then zoomed right toward him.

The minister stopped his sermon, pointed severely at his son, and commanded, "Jimmy, park the car immediately beside your mother on that bench [pointing], turn off the ignition, and hand her the keys.''

The sermon continued undisturbed—after a good laugh by the congregation.

In dealing with people, especially children, you've got to be ready for anything. Life is unpredictable.

88. Dorothy Parker (1893–1967) was a writer and wit who led a very busy life. One day she was foolish enough to accept two baby alligators as a gift. She brought them home, ran a little water in the bathtub, and put them there until she could decide what to do with them.

The next day, the cleaning woman came by while Parker was out. When Parker returned that evening, she found the house uncleaned and this note: ''Dear Madam, I am leaving. I cannot work in a house with alligators. I would have told you this before, but I never thought the subject would come up.''

No two marriages are exactly alike. But they are all marked by challenges and difficulties which can be worked out—if there's love (and humor).

89. Marriage usually is a wonderful and complicated thing. And how wonderful it is that we aren't married to people with traits just like our own! I know a couple who love each other very much but agree that one of the reasons for their happiness is what they call ''complementary stupidities.''

Another way of putting it is this: ''The rocks in *her* head seem to fit the holes in *his*.''

There are other ways to solve the married relationship.

90. A letter from Mrs. Audrey Shepherd to the *Times* of London, published March 24, 1986:

"Sir, I have done 24 jobs in the last 35 years—housekeeper, cook, cleaner, chauffeur, mother's helper, kennel maid, laundry maid, valet, shoe shine girl, window cleaner, dressmaker, upholsterer, gardener, concrete mixer, painter, decorator, plasterer, carpenter, plumber's mate, shorthand typist, telephonist, receptionist, bookkeeper, car park attendant, and, incidentally, all for one boss, my husband."

91. Many women rightfully resent husbands who refuse to have anything to do with "women's work," like housecleaning, bedmaking, or cooking anything except steaks on an outdoor barbecue. A friend of mine was especially irked by the self-righteous attitude her husband had when he actually helped with something. In a confidential moment, choosing her words carefully, she told a small group, "My husband is one who, every time he empties an ashtray, manages to convey the impression that he is required to do all the housework."

92. At the gates to heaven a new arrival, George, noted that there were two paths, one marked WOMEN, one marked MEN. He took the latter path and found that it led to two gates. The gate on the right had a sign above it: MEN WHO WERE DOMINATED BY THEIR WIVES. The sign on the left gate read: MEN WHO DOMINATED THEIR WIVES. The right-hand gate had a long line of men waiting, but there was only one scrawny little fellow at the left-hand gate. George, before he decided which gate to go to, went over to the scrawny man and asked, "Why are *you* at this gate?" The little fellow replied, "I don't know. My wife just told me to stand here."

93. Socrates (469–399 B.C.), the great Greek philosopher, was what used to be known as a henpecked husband. The "shrew" was his wife Xantippe. He is said to have once commented that having such a terrible time at home helped him become a powerful philosopher.

According to legend, one day Socrates and Xantippe had a loud argument, and finally he walked out of the door. His wife threw a bucket of water (or, in those days, it may have been something worse) on him. "After the thunder," he said, "comes the rain."

Not every man can be a Socrates. There's a simpler way to keep a marriage happy.

94. Two husbands were discussing their married lives. Although happily married, they admitted that there were arguments sometimes. Then Chad said, "I've made one great discovery. I now know how to always have the last word."

"Wow!" said Sherm, "how did you manage that?"

"It's easy," replied Chad. "My last word is always 'Yes, Dear.'"

Obviously, marriage often is not easy. Look at the divorce statistics; about half of the marriages in the United States end in divorce. Perhaps people considering marriage should be more careful.

95. As Alicia was getting to know Michael and his family, she was very impressed by how much his parents loved each other. "They're so thoughtful," Alicia said. "Why, your dad even brings your mom a cup of hot coffee in bed in the morning."

After a time, Alicia and Michael were engaged, and then married. On the way from the wedding to the reception, Alicia again remarked on Michael's loving parents, and even the coffee in bed. "Tell me," she said, "does it run in the family?"

"It sure does," replied Michael, "and I take after my mom."

And here's one about a careful, prudent, perhaps unromantic pair.

96. Stanley and his fiancée Georgette were a modern couple, quite realistic about the state of marriage these days. They met with the minister of the church to discuss their marriage vows. "Pastor," said Georgette, "we wonder if we could make a change in the wording of our ceremony."

"Yes, Georgette," replied the pastor, "it is sometimes done. What do you have in mind?"

"Well," said Georgette, looking at Stanley openly, "we'd like to alter the 'until death do us part' section to read, 'Substantial penalty for early withdrawal.' "

Once you're into it, what then?

97. A few days before her birthday a husband asked his wife, "Dear, what would you like for your present?"

Wife: I really don't think I should say.

Husband: How about a diamond ring?

Wife: I don't care much for diamonds.

Husband: Well, then, a mink coat?

Wife: You know I don't like furs.

Husband: A golden necklace?

Wife: I already have three of them.

Husband: Well, gosh, what *do* you want?

Wife: What I'd really like is a divorce.

Husband: Hmmm, I wasn't planning on spending *that* much.

It's not pleasant to think of all these divorces, but here's a creative idea suggested by a practical(?) Quaker.

98. A conscientious couple, eager to improve the world, wrote on their wedding invitation: "Please, instead of wedding gifts, send contributions to the American Friends Service Committee."

Gifts poured in to the AFSC. After a time, a person in the fund-raising department wrote the couple:

"Dear Friends,

We have received a marvelous number of large gifts for the work of the AFSC. Thank you *very* much. And I have an idea. Why don't you get divorced and then remarry? We still urgently need money for our work."

Hostility, in moderation, *can* be humorous. Of course, you can overdo it.

99. There was an irreverent wife whose husband was constantly getting himself into embarrassing situations. With a wry twinkle in her eye she told her beleaguered spouse, "To prevent putting your foot in your mouth, there are two subjects you should avoid—nouns and verbs.''

100. The wife of a fisherman was sitting on the bank of a stream reading a book while her husband fished. Someone came along and said, ''I need to speak to your husband. Can you tell me where he is?''

''Sure,'' she replied. ''Just go up the stream that-a-way and look for a pole with a worm on both ends.''

Or does it help not to have too many children? The condition has resulted in two new words.

101. Two women in their fifties were discussing a couple in their middle thirties, both of whom worked at well-paying jobs, seemed to have plenty of money, and were childless.

''You know,'' said one, ''they're just a couple of dinks.''

''Dinks?'' asked the other. ''What do you mean?''

''You know, double income, no kids—DINKS.''

(An alternative is: ''they're a diok couple—double income, one kid.'')

I didn't want to close this chapter on a negative note, but I couldn't resist a couple of somewhat off-the-wall stories.

102. A woman in need of marriage counseling went to a psychiatrist.

''And what seems to be the trouble?'' asked the psychiatrist.

''Well, my husband thinks he's a refrigerator,'' she said.

"Yes?" said the psychiatrist.

"Well," said the wife, "I suppose that's O.K., but he sleeps with his mouth open and the light keeps me awake."

103. A husband was having great difficulty getting along with his wife—nothing but arguing and friction—so he decided to consult a marriage counselor. After they had talked for a while, the counselor said, "I suggest that you run five miles each day for a week. Then please call me back."

A week later the counselor received a call from the husband. "Well," asked the counselor, "how are things going with you and your wife?"

"How should I know?" said the husband. "I'm thirty-five miles away."

So, Benjamin Franklin, we'll quote you again: "Keep your eyes wide open before marriage, half shut afterward."

4.

Language

Language, with its twists and turns, delights and horrors, comforts and shocks, is the main tool of humor. Please note that a few items in this chapter might be labeled "PG"—slightly off-color, but immensely human.

I have found it in a sense very difficult to organize these stories and collections, because language is so overlapping with itself. However, let's be brave and start with the off-color or profane stories. If you oppose such language, even though it is a real part of the human condition, turn directly to page 55.

We'll begin mildly, with some youngsters' writing.

104. These are brief excerpts from ninth-grade student writing on an English Composition Achievement Test being graded by teachers at the Educational Testing Service in Princeton, N.J. The assigned topic was: *How personalities change around different people.*

"To make yourself known, you must jiggle your personality."

"Personality change is a piece of apparatus necessary for a prolific life."

"Adultery is what adolescents are practicing for, and if we can't adjust then, when can we ever?"

"A friend is one with whom we can drop our undermost garments."

"Social climb is an everyday sport."

"At home you are as equal as night and day."

"Our homes were breeding grounds." [*Note:* A younger child, a neighbor of mine, said to me in a different context, "We come from a well-breaded family."]

"If one can't be loose with one's parents, who can one be loose with?"

"On a date a boy tries to show how masculine he is. On this point a girl can help greatly."

"Some situations warantee falsehood."

"It's nice to have a girlfriend of the opposite sex."

"He would be the acne of success."

Some of us adults think that, while it's okay for grownups to swear, children shouldn't. We should ask ourselves where the kids learn all these "bad" words.

105. Some golfers were resting beside the course when they saw a small group of boys coming along the course. The boys stopped at a sand trap and said, "Damn!" "Oh, hell!" "God!" Then they walked on to a bit of rough beside the woods, where they yelled, "Crap!" "Oh, blast it!" "Goddam!" Again the boys moved along, passing by the golfers, who were fascinated by this exhibition. One of them said, "Boys, what are you doing? You really shouldn't be talking like that."

"Well," answered one boy, "we're too young to be

allowed to play, so we're just practicing the vocabulary.''

Some young kids get into trouble using bad language when they really mean no harm at all.

106. A friend of mine was visiting a fifth-grade classroom where a boy was being tested by a remedial reading teacher. An item on the fill-in-the-blank test read, ''The cat scr__ with its claws.'' The boy wrote in the blank ''screwed.'' Then he looked up at the teacher and said, ''Man, that was some queer cat!''

A sad aspect of the above story is that the teacher whispered to my friend, ''Well, it just shows how stupid kids are, doesn't it?''
But here's another story where the ignorance is real—funny, but tragic, too.

107. A mother complained to the welfare department: ''I am very much annoyed that you have branded my boy illiterate. This is a dirty lie, as I was married a week before he was born.''

And yet another vocabulary mistake, this time from a much higher academic level.

108. A professor of economics in a widely known university in the Philadelphia area spent a period of study at Cambridge University, England. She was there at Christmas time and went to hear the famous King's College boys' choir sing. As the golden-clear voices echoed in the College chapel, she was almost overcome by the beauty. Later, back home, describing the experience to a few of us at a small party of neighbors, she said, "It was *so* beautiful; it was positively *urethral*."

People who work in religious situations or in educational administration have to watch their language with special care. Yet they have the same emotional needs as all of us.

109. A friend of mine used to be president of a Quaker college in the midwest. He had to make sure that he never used any language that might seem improper or profane. However, as any administrator of a college knows, there are times when you are very frustrated and really need to vent your feelings. My friend invented the perfect phrase to express annoyance: "Peach pits!" (Try this and see how satisfying it is.)

This college president's problem leads to a bit of information—somewhat humorous—about how our language was developed.

110. The English language is a very rich one, especially as there are two main streams in it, the Anglo-Saxon stream and the Latin stream. Thus, we can say "go up" or "ascend," "melt" or "liquefy," "kiss" or "osculate," and so forth.

But put yourself in the shoes of the Anglo-Saxons, the Germanic natives of England, after they were conquered by the Normans in 1066. The surviving natives, struggling to accommodate themselves to their aristocratic conquerers, had to stop spitting, pissing, farting, shitting, bleeding, and fucking—and begin expectorating, urinating, flatulating, sanguinating, and copulating.

And speaking of "fucking" (the word, not the activity): The word can be used to great effect and satisfaction in time of frustration or crisis. In the following story note that the *u* in "fuck" should be pronounced as we pronounce the *oo* in "took."

111. During World War II, the British Friends Ambulance Unit (FAU) transported supplies across the desert sands of North Africa. One day an FAU worker saw a British Tommy who'd got his lorry (truck) stuck in the sand. The Tommy drove the lorry forward, but it just sank deeper into the sand. He put it into reverse, and the wheels spun—even deeper. At last, after several more tries, including kicking the lorry quite hard, he backed off, put his hands on his hips, looked at the lorry with a scowl, and said, "The fuckin' fucker's fucked."

Of course, in the good old days, in any decent book the climax of this story would have been written, "The f---in' f---er's f---ed," but it seems to me better to call a sp--- a sp---.

I personally find it dull, if not offensive, to hear the words "fuck" and "fuckin' " used so much. However, using the word doesn't always mean that the user is ignorant.

112. An American serviceman was telling his pal what he had done on his overnight leave from the base. He said, "I left the fuckin' base, and waited around for a fuckin' hour or so for the fuckin' bus. Finally, it came, and we drove into the fuckin' town. I went into this fuckin' bar, and there was this fuckin' beautiful babe, so I ordered her a fuckin' drink. Well, by now we were getting pretty fuckin' friendly. We left the fuckin' bar and walked down the fuckin' main street till I saw a fuckin' little hotel, and we went in. I paid and we went up the fuckin' stairs and into this fuckin' little room.''

''Wow! Yeah?'' said his pal. ''And what did you do then?''

''We had sexual intercourse,'' said the serviceman.

Politicians have often been able to unscrupulously exploit the public's linguistic ignorance. So listen carefully!

113. When Claude Pepper (1900–1990) was running for senator from Florida in 1950, one of his opponents attacked him as follows: ''Are you aware that Claude Pepper is known all over Washington as a shameless extrovert? Not only that, but this man is reliably reported to practice nepotism with his sister-in-law, and he has a sister who once was a thespian in wicked New York City. Worst of all, it is an established fact that Mr. Pepper before his marriage habitually practiced celibacy.''

Pepper was defeated by 67,000 votes!

Foreigners, even those who are very able linquistically, often have difficulties with our rich language. Forgive me if the following story isn't as profane or off-color as the ones that surround it!

114. A South American diplomat who was stationed in the United States had developed an impressively rich English vocabulary. One day he was discussing things with a friend in the U.S. State Department, and it was obvious that he was unhappy. "You look sad," said the State Department man. "Are things not going well?"

"Well," said the diplomat, "no. I'm having trouble with my wife."

"Oh," said his friend, "that *is* bad. And I thought you loved your wife so much."

"Oh, yes," said the diplomat, "I love her very very much."

"Then what is the trouble?"

"Well," the diplomat said, "we very much want to have some children, and, er, my wife seems to be—how do you say?—*unbearable*."

"Unbearable?" asked his friend.

"No, no," said the diplomat, "I mean *inconceivable*."

Still a blank expression on his friend's face.

"What I mean, you see," said the diplomat, "is that she is—uh—oh, yes, *impregnable!*"

One can sympathize with the diplomat (although studies show that "impregnability" is usually due to *male* physical problems), but I found it harder to sympathize with the attitude of these two doctors, even while I laughed at their linguistic goof.

115. I was flying from San Francisco to Philadelphia and heard two doctors complaining to each other about some nurse's behavior. I never learned what the nurse had done, or failed to do, but it must have been bad, because one of the doctors said, "You know what I think she should do?"

"What?" asked the other.

"She should just put her head between her tail and apologize."

When I was at Harvard in 1982–83 as an Associate in Education, I used to jog rather regularly around the famous Harvard Yard. I enjoyed picking up bits of elevated conversation from the people I passed. I called them "Harvard Shards," a "shard" being a piece or fragment of something. Here's a shard that fits this chapter.

116. While jogging between the Yard and the Charles River, I overheard a young woman say to a young man, "I invited him, saying 'just wear gym shoes and a sweater,' and he took me literally."

I slowed to an inconspicuous stop to hear the response, which was: "What you mean is he literally took you."

Such linquistic and grammatical distinctions can be fun (and sometimes trying!), as is illustrated by another Harvard Shard.

117. I was trotting up the impressive marble stairway of Harvard's Widener Library when a large iron-pipe scaffolding loomed in front of me. On it a sign had been posted: "Danger! Watch your head!" Below the sign some student had magic-markered this note: "I can't see my head." Below that, another note was scribbled: "I watched my head and ran into the scaffolding."

So much for verbal distinctions. There are also grammatical rules and distinctions (or distinguishers) that lead to trouble and annoyance.

Perhaps the classic story about this is the following:

118. Winston Churchill (1874–1965), an elegant, inspiring, and powerful speaker, was going over the draft of a policy speech he had composed. As he read the draft, he noticed that some proper bureaucrat from the Foreign Office had corrected one of his eloquent sentences by moving a preposition away from the end of a sentence. Annoyed, Churchill restored the preposition to its original place and noted in the margin, "This is a form of arrant pedantry up with which I will not put."

A less noble but equally effective rebuttal to the preposition rule was uttered by a little boy.

119. The mother in a family that objected very much to the narrow grammar teaching given by the local school was delighted by an example of fine, clear English used in her house. At school, they taught that one must *never* end a sentence with a preposition. Well, one evening, just after supper, while her husband was washing the dishes, she prepared to put her son to bed and to read aloud to him. She got a book they had been struggling through a bit, and came to the bottom of the stairs. The little boy looked down, saw the book she had in her hand, and asked in a plain, clear voice, "Mom, what are you bringing that book I don't want to be read to out of up for?"

Some people fervently believe that teaching everybody Latin is the way to cure the grammatical errors of writers of English, even though the two grammars are quite different, Latin relying heavily on inflection, English on word order. Be that as it may (and some believers are so

grim about it that it's not even funny), Latin can be fun.
Here are two examples, the first a little bit noble, despite
the bilingual puns, the second totally *ig*noble if not *ig*-
norant.

120. In an old Catholic mystery play, all the birds and
animals were represented in the nativity scene. The
creatures spoke thus, in Latin, of course.

The cock: Christus natus est! (Christ is born.)
The duck: Quando? Quando? (When? When?)
The dog: Hac nocte, hac nocte. (Tonight, tonight.)
The cows: Ubi? Ubi? (Where? Where?)
The lambs: Bethlehem, Bethlehem.

121. A nephew of mine, a Catholic, knows a little
Latin and claims that it's useful. "It helps you remember important things," he said.

"Like what?" I asked.

"Like 'Semper ubi sub ubi,' " replied my nephew.

"Well, I know those words, I think. *Semper* means
'always'; *ubi* means 'where'; and *sub* means 'under.'
But what's that got to do with important things?"

"When you're getting dressed in the morning, just
say 'Semper ubi sub ubi': 'Always wear underwear.' "

Now let's move to another area of language: delightful
goofs.

122. In the play *The Rivals* by Richard B. Sheridan
(1751–1816), there is a character named Mrs. Malaprop, the aunt and guardian of Lydia Languish, who
was noted for her aptitude for misapplying words. An
example: "As headstrong as an allegory on the banks

of the Nile." Her name derives from the French *mal à propos*, "out of place." In his *New York Times* column "On Language," November 8, 1981, William Safire invented a related expression, *boniprop*, which is a malaprop that is especially apt, especially good—*bon*, not *mal*. In the column in which he coined the word, Safire gave as examples: "Richard Nixon . . . avoided impeachment by a hare's breath"; a Soviet general arrived in Poland "in a tight security blanket"; "a forlorn conclusion"; and "fuming at the mouth."

Even though Oscar Wilde (1854–1900) said that "the only way to get rid of a temptation is to yield to it," I have resisted the temptation to make a whole chapter of this book consist entirely of the malaprops and boniprops I've been collecting ever since Safire's column, because, after all, this is a treasury of humorous stories about the human condition. However, since a part of our condition is to twist, turn, and tangle the English language in delightful ways—sometimes as a way of masking tragedy—I give below a very few of the best, some by people whose native language is English, some by those who learned English later in life.

By native speakers of English

- "All they do is sit around in meetings and postulate."
- "My brother is on the football team, and he's an offensive throwback."—sixth-grade girl.
- "That freak, he's always hurling epitaphs at people."—an official of a large city speaking of a civil liberties activist. (He should have said *epithets*.)
- "We're investigating. We're going to find out if they're really sick or only philandering."—the po-

lice commissioner of a large city. (The word he
should have used is *malingering*.)

- "I wouldn't eat it with a ten-foot pole."
- "My advice is, use your own discrepancy."
- "Yeah, it was a real cliff-dweller."—baseball team
  manager describing a close game.
- "I've got a gut feeling off the top of my head."—a
  Yale graduate and major in English!
- "The worm has turned, and the shoe is on the other
  foot."—a U.S. Congressman.
- "My friend has a bad case of spinal-moanin'-Jesus."
  (spinal meningitis.)
- "Well, the team sort of flew off on a handle."—
  football team manager, about his team not following
  game plans.
- "I need to think about it. Let me regurgitate for a
  couple of hours."—an executive after hearing a
  complicated question.

By non-native speakers of English

- "Thank you, sir, for this kind wastage of your
  time."
- "Sir, I thank you from the heart of my bottom."
- "From here it will be about five miles as the cock
  crows."
- Football player to referee: "You bloody damn. I'll
  blow your nose."
- "I am a simple man. I speak what is in my mind. I
  have nothing in my behind."
- "As I went under for a second time, my whole pos-
  terior passed before me in a flash."—a man who
  narrowly escaped drowning.
- "In these hard times, my wife and I have been burn-

ing the candle at both ends, but are hard put to it to make our both ends meet."

- "My learned friend's case is nothing but a tissue of piffles."—one lawyer to the judge about the opposing lawyer.

And here are two more boniprops that deserve special attention

- An architectural colleague of my daughter used to have original ways of describing almost any person or happening. About a useful and powerful person he knew, he said, "He's really a landmine of information." And when he had had a long and vigorous telephone conversation with this person, somewhat overheard in the small office, he hung up at last and said to those nearby, "Well, I really gave him a piece of my ear."
- A different boniprop user, a top executive of a group of schools, had been quite bothered by a heavy problem. One day he came into the office seeming much more cheerful. When people commented, he explained, "Well, I let my hair down and got it off my chest."

Before we get to the weighty subject of insurance, let's look at a few more apt uses, or misuses of our language.

123. A man got sick and his friend asked him what was the matter. "It's something to do with my kidleys," he said.

"You mean kidneys, don't you?" asked his friend.

The sick man replied, "I said 'kidleys,' diddle I?"

124. A man entered a restaurant on the banks of the Chesapeake Bay, sat down, and looked rather impatient and grouchy. At last a waiter appeared.

"It's about time!" said the man. "Now tell me. Do you serve crabs here?"

"Certainly, sir," replied the waiter, "we serve anyone."

125. "Well," said a skeptic after hearing a very complicated explanation of a situation, "the whole thing reminds me of the man who crossed an abalone with a crocodile."

"Yeah?" asked a friend.

"Yeah," said the man. "He hoped he'd get an abadile. But instead he got a crockabaloney."

And now to insurance. Some people will say or write anything to show that they are not at fault.

126. Insurance companies get some rather strange descriptions of auto accidents when people make their claims. Here are a few:

- "The other car collided with mine without giving warning of its intentions."
- "I thought my window was down but found it was up when I put my hand through it."
- "I collided with a stationary truck coming the other way."
- "A pedestrian hit me and went under my car."
- "The guy was all over the road. I had to swerve a number of times before I hit him."
- "I pulled away from the side of the road, glanced at my mother-in-law, and headed over the embankment."

- "In my attempt to kill a fly I drove into a telephone pole."
- "I was on my way to the doctor with rear end trouble when my universal joint gave way, causing me to have an accident."
- "An invisible car came out of nowhere, struck my vehicle, and vanished."
- "The pedestrian had no idea which way to run, so I ran over him."
- "The telephone pole was approaching. I was attempting to swerve out of the way when it struck my front end."

I spent a delightful part of my life teaching sixth grade—a noble task, but one that carries some risks, to wit:

127. A result of my teaching sixth grade is a collection of a number of bits that my wife labels "sixth-grade humor." The following examples must be used selectively—only with certain groups who are not allergic to corn. There are two categories, (1) "What did the X say to the X?" and (2) "What was said when . . . ?" or "What happened when . . . ?"

Category 1:

- What did one toe say to another?
  Don't look now, but I think we're being followed by a heel.
- What did one eye say to the other?
  There's something between us that smells.
- What did one wall say to another?
  I'll meet you at the corner.

- What did the carpet say to the floor?
  Gotcha covered!
- What did the little termite say to his father? (They were in a pub.)
  Beat me, Daddy, I ate the bar. [*Note:* This joke derives from the boogie-woogie percussive piano piece, "Beat Me, Daddy, Eight to the Bar."]
- One ant was running across an unopened box of crackers and urging another to speed up. "But why do we have to hurry?" said one. "Can't you read, you nut? It says, 'Tear along the dotted line.' "

Category 2:

- What did the sparrow say when it was run over by a Model T?
  Cheap! Cheap!
- What happened when the sparrow flew into the electric fan?
  Shredded tweet.
- What did the monkey say when it backed into the lawnmower?
  It won't be long now. [*Note:* Less genteel version: They're off!]
- What happened when the woman was pushed backward into an airplane propellor?
  Disaster.

Now, it may seem like quite a transition to go from sixth-grade humor to a complex, culture-filled special form of American dialect—and it is. One is rather simple; the other is beautifully complex and tinged with deep understanding of the human condition.

128. A wonderful, vivid, eloquent language that was spoken widely in the South a generation or two ago, but is not spoken so much today, enriches the American culture. Here are some charming bits and phrases that were told by a faithful friend now well into her seventies. She explains that they were used mainly, but not only, by Negroes. (She strongly resists the label "black.")

- Mrs. Washington, who wasn't feeling well, was asked, "How are you?" Her reply: "I ain't no great big thing." She could also have said, "Fair to middlin', considerin'."

- Yet another person described his troubles thus: "I got a little botheration in the knee and a little worryation in the head." [*Note:* These, of course, remind us of Joel Chandler Harris's (1848–1908) phrase, a way to ask "How are you?": How's yo' symptoms sagatuatin'?"]

- And a mother with several young children exclaimed, "If those children keep that racket up, they'll be in the hospital and I'll be in jail." This mother, evidently, didn't have a temper "as slow as molasses running uphill in winter."

- A classic retort was made to the washing machine repairman who kept promising to come to fix the washer, yet never came. The next time he promised, the housewife replied, "I'm sick of you pissin' in my face and callin' it rain."

129. An even richer collection of delights of Old South language is found in *Their Eyes Were Watching God*, by Zora Neals Hurston (1900–1960), published by the University of Illinois Press in 1937 and again in 1978. Here are some bits I've selected. Read the book!

Derogatory comment about small size of a town, place, property, etc.: "Y'ain't got enough room here to cuss a cat on without gittin' yo' mouf full of hair."

About a bossy fat man: "All he do is big-belly round and tell other folks what to do." "Dat chastisin' feelin' he totes sorter gives yuh de protolapsis uh de cutinary linin'." "He's uh whirlwind among breezes."

About an underfed mule: "Dat mule so skinny till de women is usin't his rib bones fuh uh rub-board, and hangin' things out on his hock-bones tuh dry."

About a liar: "You'se a stinkin' lie, and yo' feet ain't mates."

About people not talking about something: "Dey's mighty hushmouf about it."

To a storekeeper who gives some food to a hungry woman for her family: "You's du most gentlemanified man Ah ever did see. You'se uh king!"

Reply of a person who said she'd never learned something because "it wuz too heavy fuh mah brains": "But you got good meat on yo' head. You'll learn."

I don't want to gossip about it: "Ah ain't puttin' it in de street. Ah'm tellin' you."

Reply meaning, "I won't tell": "Ah jus lak chicken. Chicken drink water, but he don't pee-pee."

Please keep it secret: "We ain't shamefaced. We jus' ain't ready tuh make no big kerflummock as yet."

About a white person's hair: "She got meriny skin and hair jus' as close tuh her head as ninety-nine is tuh uh hundred."

A proper punishment for someone who's done something bad: "He oughta be tried and sentenced tuh six months behind de United States privy house at hard smellin'."

I suppose we can't know too many languages and dialects—the more the richer. (We should know at least two.)

130. A mother mouse and her three children crept out of their hole into the kitchen and began feasting on some delicious bits of food. Suddenly, out of the corner of her eye, Mother Mouse saw a cat slinking toward them. The cat was between the mice and their hole. The mother mouse puffed up her lungs and went, "Woof! Woof!" The cat turned tail and ran.

With that, the mother quickly led her children back to safety in their hole. When they were settled and breathing normally, Mother Mouse said to her children, "Now, what's the lesson from that experience?"

"We don't know," the baby mice squeaked.

"It is this," said Mom Mouse. "It's good to know a second language."

Sometimes language comes in delightful short masterpieces.

131. The best example of a *short* suspense story, a total tragedy, is the following classic, the origin of which I cannot discover.

> Benjie met a bear.
> The bear was bulgy,
> The bulge was Benjie.

132. Who else but Ogden Nash (1902–1971) could have written this following irreverent bit on the subject of reproduction?

> Whales have calves,
> Cats have kittens,

Bears have cubs,
Bats have bittens,
Swans have cygnets,
Seals have puppies,
But guppies just have little guppies.

And mixed metaphors—boniprops?—are nice, especially when unintentional.

133. A third-grade boy I knew, who got into trouble from time to time, was in the principal's office for a quiet talking-to.

"And Ted," asked the principal, "how do you like your teacher? Do you get along all right?"

"Oh, yes," replied Ted. "I think she's the cream of the coop."

But there are intentional metaphors, delightful combinations of images.

134. The mother of E. M. Forster (1879–1970) was named Alice Wichelo, or "Lily." She had an old friend, Mrs. Mawe, whom she was said to love very much. One day she stated, "At times, much as I love Mrs. Mawe, I could tear her to ribbons and use a chopper besides. She tosses erroneous statements in the air like an aimless cow."

The strongest condemnation I ever heard of an erroneous statement was made by an eleventh-grade neighbor of mine (and my candidate for the first woman president of the United States, although she won't be old enough until 2002).

135. An adolescent girl, when she was told that some-one had accused her class of prejudice against blacks and Jews, replied with fire in her eye and voice: "That statement about my class is the ultimate of notness."

136. A well-known line from Shakespeare's *Richard III* is: "Now is the winter of our discontent." (Act 1, sc.1, 1.1) Not long ago a sales poster was seen in a clothing store window in Brighton, England, reading, NOW IS THE SUMMER OF OUR DISCOUNT PANTS.

137. Some signs we human beings write are uninten-tionally humorous. Of the hundreds I've collected over the years, here are a few which, in their twisted way, give special delight. The first group is by native speak-ers of English, the second by non-native speakers. Of course, some, you'll see, are not unintentional—quite the contrary.

Signs by people whose native language is English

- Announcements or notices seen on church bulletin boards:

    "This afternoon there will be a meeting in the south and north ends of the church. Children will be baptized at both ends."

    "On Wednesday, the Ladies' Liturgy Society will

meet. Mrs. Johnson will sing, 'Put Me in My Little Bed,' accompanied by the Pastor.''

"Thursday, 5 P.M., Little Mothers Club. All those wishing to become Little Mothers, please meet the Pastor in his study.''

- The morning calendar posted on a bulletin board at Friends House, a Quaker center, Euston Road, London:

> 9:00 National Eczema Society
> 9:30 Natural Combine
> 11:00 Baden-Powell Scouts
> 12:30 Schizophrenia

- Notice on the fence of a small church graveyard:

"As the maintenance of the churchyard is becoming increasingly costly, it would be appreciated if those who are willing would clip the grass around their own graves.''

- On the freight platform of a large station stood a hefty carton on which was printed:

> TO AVOID BREAKAGE
> KEEP BOTTOM ON TOP.

Underneath this, a slightly smaller sign had been pasted:

> TOP MARKED BOTTOM
> TO AVOID CONFUSION.

- In Harrod's department store in London:

> PLEASE TRY NOT TO SMOKE.

- On a small warehouse beside the River Thames:

> NO SMOKING IN CASE OF FIRE.

- On the IN and OUT boxes of the desk of an executive of a poultry company:

> COCK-A-DOODLE-DO   COCK-A-DOODLE-DONE

- Sign posted on a desk in the U.S. Customs House, Philadelphia:

Rate Schedule

Answers $1.00
Answers That Require Thought $2.00
Correct Answers $4.00
Dumb Looks Are Still Free.

- Sign in a microstudy medical research office, Sheffield, England: "People who think they know everything are particularly annoying to those of us who do."
- In a plumbing supply store: "Don't be afraid to ask dumb questions. That way you won't make dumb mistakes."
- In the large space between the top of the chalkboard and the ceiling, in an eighth-grade classroom, the teacher had posted a sign which said in very large letters:

IT'S SAFE TO MAKE A MISTAKE IN THIS CLASSROOM

—which is a very fine educational idea. Under the large sign, however, in smaller letters, was printed: ". . . but more to your credit to make a different one each time."
- Rules worked out by members of an eight-year-olds' club and posted on their treehouse:

CLUB RULES (Obay)

1. Be friends together.
2. No sudden moves.
3. Peaceful wars.
4. Unpeaceful wars if necessary.
5. Gim practice every day.
6. Help each other if necessary.
7. No teasing at all.
8. If running away do not chass.

Signs by people whose native language is not English

- Notice in safari park in Kenya: "Visitors who throw litter into crocodile pit will be asked to retrieve it."
- Posted conspicuously in the zoo in Colombo, Sri Lanka:

  "If you will litter with disgrace
  And spoil the beauty of this place,
  May indigestion wrack your chest
  And ants invade your pants and vest."

- Leaflet from car-leasing company in Tokyo: "When a passenger of foot heave in sight, tootle the horn. Trumpet at him melodiously first, but if he still obstacles your passage then tootle him with vigor!"
- Notice in Japanese hotel room: "Is forbitten to steal the hotel towels please. If you are not person to do such thing please not to read notis."
- Hong Kong dentist advertisement: "Teeth extracted by latest Methodists."
- Posted in elevator in Belgrade, capital of Yugoslavia: "To move cabin push button for wishing floor. If the cabin should enter more persons, each one should press number of wishing floor. Driving is then going alphabetically by national order."
- In tailor's shop in Jordan: "Order your summers suit. Because is big rush we will execute customers in strict rotation."

So, dear reader, you are executed—fairly. Let's go on to human manners.

5.

Manners—Good, Bad, and Unintentional

Manners can delight us, revolt us, or make us feel rejected. Are they a basis for civilized behavior—or merely for self-satisfaction? Ralph Waldo Emerson (1803–1882) defined manners as "a contrivance . . . to keep fools at a distance"; and Mark Twain (1835–1910) commented: "Training is everything. The peach was once a bitter almond; the cauliflower is . . . nothing but a cabbage with a college education."

We should perhaps begin by citing Mark Twain's irreverent view of manners.

138. Mark Twain was not very particular about how he dressed, and he was frequently criticized by his wife for visiting people without wearing a collar and tie. One day, after Twain had returned from a neighbor's, his spouse was particularly annoyed by his informal dress. Twain marched upstairs, wrapped a collar and tie in a neat package, and had a local boy deliver it to the neighbor's house, with this note attached: "I visited you without a collar or tie for approximately a half-hour. The missing articles are enclosed. Will you kindly gaze at them for a half-hour to appease my wife, then return them to me.''

Now to the basics of manners.

139. Here is a nine-year-old boy's essay on an assigned topic.

Good Manners:
''I have good manners. I say good night and good morning and hello and goodby and please and thank you, and when I see anything dead lying around the house I bury it.''

And perhaps children can teach us adults a thing or two.

140. A teacher observed a boy entering the classroom—his hands were dirty. She stopped him and said, ''John, please wash your hands. My goodness, what would you say if I came into the room with hands like that?''

With a smile the boy replied, ''I think I'd be too polite to mention it.''

Notice the rather tactful way the boy put the teacher down—a smile, and an ''I think.'' It's good to be tactful; it's good to be polite.

141. Here is an experience that illustrates the subtle difference between politeness and tact. A window washer was making his way around an apartment building in Philadelphia when suddenly he found himself looking right at a completely nude woman taking a bath. He said, "Excuse me, sir." Now, the "excuse me" was politeness; the "sir" was tact.

Sometimes people who rise to high positions in our American institutions manage, with tact and wit, to be insulting to each other—even in the armed forces and the church.

142. Two college classmates were friends but also highly competitive, each always trying to outdo or humble the other. They both did well in life, one in the navy, one in the church. The naval man became an admiral, and wore his much-decorated uniform with great pride. The churchman became a bishop and always wore colorful ecclesiastical robes.

After they had not seen each other for some years, they happened to meet at the doorway of a fancy hotel in Philadelphia. They recognized each other but did not let on. Instead, the bishop walked over to the admiral, tapped him on the shoulder, and said, "Pardon me, doorman, but could you please hail me a taxi for the station?"

The admiral turned, looked the bishop up and down, and answered very graciously, "Madame, in your condition, do you think you should be traveling?"

I feel sure that the admiral and bishop had a good laugh after their competitive insults. Otherwise, they never would have risen as high as they did. But there are some ways in which the lowliest person and the greatest are equal.

143. The English novelist George Eliot (1819–1880), who knew about high and mighty people, said, "There are conditions under which the most majestic person is obliged to sneeze.''

Sneezing leads rather gracefully into another aspect of manners—what to do about bodily explosions. Reader, beware! The next few stories may verge on the off-color.

144. A friend of mine belonged to a health club, where he and some other men went during lunch hour and exercised strenuously. A nearly inevitable part of this exercise was flatulation, or, to use the plain Anglo-Saxon word, *farting*. In the gym, the men farted freely in each other's company.

Then a woman joined the group, and an amazing thing happened: All the farting stopped at once. She remained a part of the club for a few months and then was transferred to another branch, so the farting recommenced. However, after more than a year—and by now I think it was about 1978, and times were changing—two women joined the club. The men were somewhat abashed and prepared to recommence self-control, but, lo and behold, both the women, as they went through their paces, farted freely, and the men started, too, and there was free coeducational farting.

But such problems can arise even in situations where only women are involved. The following story also suggests a hazard of patriotism and its ceremonial aspects.

145. Mrs. Grace, Mrs. Rock, and Mrs. Powell were invited to visit the beautiful new home of Mrs. Kelly. Mrs. Kelly took special pains to tell her friends to look around carefully when they went to the bathroom upstairs. Mrs. Grace finally excused herself and visited the bathroom. She came down a bit tardily and in a state of excitement, saying, "My dears, when I sat down it played Beethoven!"

Mrs. Rock then felt the need and hurried to the second floor. She returned all glowing, saying, "I sat down and it played *The Unfinished Symphony.*"

Mrs. Powell was last. She didn't come down, however. After fifteen minutes had passed, Mrs. Kelly grew worried and went upstairs. There was Mrs. Powell on the floor wiping it up.

"What happened?" gasped Mrs. Kelly.

"Just my luck," said Mrs. Powell. "When I sat down, it played the 'Star-Spangled Banner'."

It's perhaps a major social leap to go from an elegant bathroom to a public toilet or privy, but they do have some things in common.

146. Graffiti written inside men's rooms have a certain humor to them. Here are two I've seen so often they could be called classics:

- A man's ambition is mighty small
  Who writes his name on a shit house wall.
- Our aim is to keep this place clean.
  Your aim will help.

A third was sent to me by an older friend. Written above a men's urinal: "If you shake it more than three times, you're playing with it." Said my oldster: "This does not apply to me."

Something I've never had the opportunity to observe nor the courage to ask is: *What* is written in ladies' (women's) rooms? Are women less articulate and literary than men? More discreet? Please, readers, share with me any specifics so that I may pass the words along. Write to E. W. Johnson, 6110 Ardleigh St., Philadelphia, PA 19138.

Now, while we are still in the slightly-off-color (SOC) mode, let's consider a mannerly exchange with literary aspects.

147. A businessman was walking through Rittenhouse Square in Philadelphia when a ragged-looking bum stopped him and said, "Buddy, can you spare a quarter?"

The businessman, a well-read type, replied, "I'm sorry, no. 'Neither a borrower nor a lender be.'—Shakespeare."

The bum glared and said, " 'Fuck you.'—Tennessee Williams."

The Shakespeare quotation is from *Hamlet*, Act 1, Scene 3. Where the Williams quote is from I do not know, and I doubt whether the bum did either.

Now we shall turn to some stories about manners and children.

148. A Cub Scout troop was half an hour late to its den meeting. The den mother asked them severely, "Why are you so late?"

"Oh," said one boy, "we were helping an old man cross the street."

"That's a nice thing for Scouts to do," said the mother. She paused. "But it shouldn't make you half an hour late."

"Well, you see," said another boy, "he didn't want to go."

149. Young Jean was having dinner at a friend's house, and the friend's mother, wanting to be sure everything went all right, asked the girl, ''Do you like spinach?''

''Oh, yes,'' replied Jean, ''I love it.''

So the mother served spinach, along with other good things, but toward the end of dinner she noticed that Jean's plate was empty, except for the spinach.

''What's the matter, Jean?'' said the mother. ''I thought you said you loved spinach.''

''Oh, I do,'' Jean explained, ''but not enough to eat it.''

150. Perhaps the worst put-down a guest could give a host is to say, on departing, ''I've had a very nice evening—but this wasn't it.'' Maybe a more ladylike departing word would be, ''Don't think it hasn't been charming, because it hasn't.'' But the child's version of the same sort of ill manners, beautifully naive, is the comment one little girl made upon leaving a birthday party: ''My mommy told me to say I had a good time.''

151. A painter who was part of the maintenance department at Sidwell Friends School in Washington shares this experience. As he was painting a door and being watched by eighth-grade Sandy, he asked, ''Do you like this school?''

''Well, no, not much,'' replied Sandy.

The painter: ''How come?''

Sandy: ''Aw, it's the kids. They're all a bunch of snobs.''

Painter: ''Really?''

Sandy: ''Yeah.''

Painter: ''Well, you go here. Are you a snob?''

Sandy: "Do you think I'd stand here talking to a painter if I were?"

Now, more about snobs. Don't let the fact that two of these stories took place in Philadelphia let you think that we Philadelphians think that we are better than others. We're far too intelligent for that.

152. At a Friday afternoon Philadelphia Orchestra concert in the famed Academy of Music, mainly attended by older and fashionable Main Line and Chestnut Hill ladies, a young man with sneakers and very long brown hair sat near the front of the orchestra section, beside a rather snooty looking lady. After they had both read their programs for a few minutes, she turned to the fellow, looked down her nose, and said, "Young man, are you an habitué of these concerts?"

"No, Madame," he replied, "I'm a son of a habitué."

153. A friend of mine who lives near the somewhat aristocratic community of Chestnut Hill recently bought some utterly delicious thin, crisp sugar cookies at the Women's Exchange there. She came back a few days later to buy some more, and when she said how scrumptious they were, the saleslady asked, "Do you know *why* they're so good?" My friend asked why. "Because," said the woman, "they're made by *ladies*."

154. At a rather exclusive club in Minneapolis, a Very Important Member received what he considered rather casual and off-hand service from a new steward. The member shouted, "Do you know who I am?"

"No sir," replied the steward, "but I will make inquiries and then come and tell you."

155. A high-society lady felt very much embarrassed that her daughter ran off and married a man who had no social position but had lots of money. One day she introduced her new son-in-law to some friends, and she winced as he talked to them in language that was neither grammatical nor refined. When he had left the room for a short time, the lady said in a low voice, "Well, you know, even the most fertile lands must be manured from time to time."

We Americans sometimes think that the English are a bit snobbish. Well, my wife and I have spent quite a lot of time in the United Kingdom, and I can tell you that we were always graciously received and treated, even by a knight or two. The British (some of them) do have a sound sense of social propriety, though.

156. It happened at Cambridge University, England, on the River Cam, shortly after women were permitted to punt their boats on the river. An all-male crew was punting and, unfortunately, upset. The men all climbed out of the boat and the river and took off their clothes to dry themselves. They were standing there, nude, when a women's crew approached. All of the men quickly wrapped jerseys or towels around their loins, except for one man who wrapped his towel around his head and face.

After the women had passed by, the men all turned on the fellow who'd covered his head. "What did you do that for, you fool?"

"Well," said the crewman, "in the social circles in

which I move, people are generally recognized by their faces.''

And, of course, there *are* class distinctions—which one little London girl didn't properly recognize.

157. As an act of charity, the wife of a local magistrate in a poor district of London invited a little girl from the area to tea. The girl sat down at the tea table, looked around, and then turned to her hostess. ''I see you keep your house very clean,'' she said. ''Cleanliness is next to godliness, you know.''

The magistrate's wife smiled at the girl and winked at her husband.

The little girl went on. ''Is your husband working?''

''Of course he is!'' said the lady. ''Why do you ask such a strange question?''

The girl continued. ''And are you both keeping off the drink?''

''Why, what an impertinent little girl you are!'' cried the lady. ''When you are invited to tea, you should try to behave like a lady, my child.''

''Oh, but I am trying,'' replied the little girl. ''When ladies visit our house, they always ask these questions.''

''Keeping off the drink''—something a world-famous head of state did not wish to do.

158. Winston Churchill (1874–1965) lived to a ripe old age despite (or perhaps because of) his smoking and drinking, which he very much enjoyed. Once he was seated beside a lady at dinner. She observed his be-

havior, screwed up her courage, and said, "Mr. Churchill, you're drunk."

Churchill replied, "Madame, *you're* ugly. And
tomorrow, *I'll* be sober."

Here are some other ways to manage—with manners—
the intake of alcohol.

159. It's interesting to observe human behavior when
the wine is passed around at a dinner party. There are
three types of people. The first put their hands directly
on top of their glass, clearly showing they want no
more. The second drain their glass quickly so that there
will be no doubt that they want more. However, the
third are more subtle: As the pourer comes near, they
quickly look away and become engaged in conversation so that they will get some more without having to
admit they want it.

Good manners can be carried to extremes, and sometimes we are unaware of the underlying mechanisms involved. Here is an example far removed from wine at
dinner.

160. An American diplomat was speaking to a large
crowd at a public meeting in Abidjan, Ivory Coast,
Africa. Out of respect for the audience, and for the
interpreter, he spoke slowly. He also told some jokes,
likewise very slowly. After each joke, he was amazed
how the translator used only a few words to make the
crowd roar with laughter.

Afterwards the diplomat asked the interpreter,
"How did you manage to tell each joke so rapidly?"

"Oh, it's easy," said the interpreter. "I just say: 'He told a joke. Laugh!' "

We near the end of manners, or at least this chapter on manners. Here are two stories to help you move on into the sometimes heavier subject of schools, education, and teachers. The first has to do with mental capacity, actual or supposed.

161. A too-wise guy was given the following piece of advice by a good friend: "It's better to remain silent and be thought stupid than to open your mouth and forever remove all doubt."

And last is a delightful retort. Perhaps it is also an educational exchange from school to parent.

162. Horace Taft, head of the Taft School in Watertown, Conn., some time back in the 20s expelled a boy from the school for repeatedly breaking the rules and engaging in bad behavior. The boy's father was outraged and wrote to Taft: "You seem to think you can run this school any way you damn please."

Taft replied: "Your manners are vulgar and your language is coarse, but you seem to have grasped the main idea."

6

Education, Schools, and Teachers

We've all been educated to a greater or worse extent, and much of that education took place in schools, done by teachers—members of the world's noblest profession. And what is education?

163. Kenneth Johnson (no relation) provided one of the most profound definitions of education that I know: "Education is proceeding from cocksure ignorance to thoughtful uncertainty." (Isn't that a bit like Sir Isaac Newton's [1642–1727] idea that human knowledge is an island in a vast sea of the unknown? For, said Newton, the larger the island grows, the longer its coastline.)

And Henry David Thoreau (1817–1862) also criticizes education: "What does education often do? It makes a straight-cut ditch out of a free, meandering brook."

But Dr. Samuel Johnson (1709–1784) (also no relation) would disagree. No meandering brooks for him!: "There is now less flogging in our great schools than formerly—but then less is learned there, so that what the boys get at one end they lose at the other."

I'm not sure I can go along with Johnson, S., but I

can with T. S. Eliot (1885–1965), who wrote, "So
many of us in our day suppose that we are emancipated
when really we are merely unbuttoned."

Some youngsters have a delightfully secure idea of education and its progress.

164. It had been a fine year in third grade and the
children were saying goodbye to the teacher on the last
day. Little Janey asked, "Can you answer one last
question?"

"Of course, Janey," said the teacher. "What is it?"

"Well," said Janey, "we're at the end of third grade.
Do I now know half as much as I don't know?"

Before we look at some more ideas children have about
education and knowledge, let's look again at Sir Isaac
Newton, a great man who saw himself as a child in some
ways.

165. During an eighteen-month period in his early
twenties, Sir Isaac Newton (1642–1727) invented theories of gravity, light, and color, as well as calculus.
At age 85, shortly before his death, he wrote, "I do
not know what I may appear to the world, but to myself I have been only like a boy playing on the sea-
shore, and diverting myself in now and then finding a
smoother pebble or a prettier shell, whilst the great
ocean of truth lay all undiscovered before me."

We must grant that not all children are as wise as the
85-year-old Newton, but they do express bits of wisdom
or simple logic.

166. A little girl complained that she didn't want to go back to school.

"But why, Jenny?" asked her mother.

"Well, I can't read, I can't write, and they won't let me talk."

167. A younger girl adjusted less logically to the rigors of arithmetic. She refused to go back to school the third day because, "Yesterday they told me that 2 + 2 equals 4 and today it's 3 + 1."

Children even express some logic that is not so simple. I submit that the girl quoted below was a profound thinker.

168. A fifth-grade teacher was giving a lesson in arithmetic. She asked the children to explain on paper how you know when to add, subtract, divide, or multiply. Here is one girl's paper:

"If there are lots of numbers, you add. If there are only two numbers, with lots of parts, you subtract. But if there are just two numbers, and one is a little harder than the other, then it is a hard problem, so you divide, *if* they come out even, but if they don't, you multiply."

Children in school come up with some wonderfully effective ways of dealing with school requirements.

169. In an elementary school art class, the students were told to draw a dog. The children went to work. A visitor came in and complimented a girl on her excellent drawing. The girl looked at the visitor and said quite earnestly, "I really can't draw a dog. So when I have to have a dog, I just draw a horse, and it always looks like a dog.''

This sort of self-confidence also goes over into the field of spelling.

170. A young girl said to her friend after a spelling test, ''Sure, I know how to spell *banana*, but I just don't know when to stop.''

To continue this section on schools, here is a marvelous message of praise from a group of children, written by a fourth grader.

171. One morning a school principal, Mr. Jackson, came into his office and found a jar of something green in the middle of his desk. A note, in careful, childish handwriting, was attached:

''Dear Mr. Jackson,

Our class was making applesauce. Some of it we are giving to Miss Dunster [head of the lower school]. Some we are giving to other people we think deserve applesauce. We think you especially deserve some applesauce, and so we are sending you a quart of applesauce.''

Sincerely yours,
Paul McKoy

I quoted this letter in my ''Gadfly'' column for the bulletin of the National Association of Independent Schools and I learned later that many school heads had it Xeroxed and put copies in each teacher's mailbox. We all need praise, even (perhaps especially) heads of schools, who too often are seen as having an easy life behind a desk in a big office, never facing reality. Take it from me, who headed a large school for a few years, "Give heads applesauce!"

Here's an extreme example of where a board of trustees refused to praise the head, or even accept praise of him. Obviously, the story is apocryphal, but there's much truth in the Apocrypha.

172. As a part of a vacation arranged by a member of his board of trustees, the headmaster of a very prestigious American school was able not only to have an audience with the Pope but to go on a short boat trip with His Eminence. During the trip, a gust of wind blew the Pope's white hat off, and the headmaster climbed over the rail, walked across the water, got the hat, and returned it to His Eminence.

The Pope was impressed, and when he returned to the Vatican he wrote a note to the school's Board of Trustees, reporting on the event. Some time later, the Pope received this reply: "Thank you, Your Eminence, for informing the Board of Trustees that our headmaster is unable to swim."

Principals (and other officials) of schools must be tactful in order to avoid needless trouble, but it's a temptation for them to insert small barbs of wit into what they say or write.

173. Schoolteachers and principals often feel that they must try to say something favorable about students who really aren't doing that well. Thus, one principal wrote on a report card, "This boy, I fear, does his best."

And a grade adviser, required to write a reference for a younger student in connection with a summer job, wrote, "Conduct generally good." This prospective employer called up to ask for more specifics. "Who do you mean, 'Generally'?" he asked.

"Oh," said the grade adviser, " 'not particularly.' "

Principals also spend a good deal of time visiting classes and evaluating teachers' performance. Often these activities do not bring them much popularity.

174. A school principal was visiting classes in his school. After spending half an hour in Mr. Montgomery's ninth-grade class, he was not very well impressed and asked the teacher to see him in the office after school.

Mr. Montgomery arrived, and the principal suggested quite a few ways in which he might improve his performance. Mr. Montgomery said, angrily, "Sir, how can you say all these things? Don't you know that I've had twenty year's experience?"

The principal replied, "I'm sorry, Mr. Montgomery. You haven't had twenty years' experience. You've had one year's experience, twenty times over."

Related to this comment is a disease that some elderly—and some not-so-elderly—people sometimes develop: hardening of the categories.

175. This scene took place in a school principal's office:

Principal: I'm afraid, Miss Levie, there's too much emphasis on the three R's in your classroom.

Miss Levie: But, sir, the three R's are absolutely basic.

Principal: And what are the three R's?

Miss Levie: Why reading, writing, and arithmetic, of course.

Principal: The trouble is that in your classroom, Miss Levie, they seem to be *rote routine response*.

(Better than the three R's, I think, are the *four* R's: reading, writing, reckoning, and reasoning—first thought up by John Esty, head of the National Association of Independent Schools.)

The most classic example of administration and educational self-confidence and egotism, carried, perhaps to the point of puffed ignorance is this statement touting the virtues of a school.

176. J. M. Ray was the head of Germantown Academy, near Philadelphia. He founded the school in 1794. He was not a modest man, being the author of these two works: *Comprehensive View of Philosophical, Political, and Theological Systems, from Creation to the Present Time;* and *Only True Guide to the English Grammar.* In his catalog he stated that the curriculum included "French, Latin, Greek, Hebrew, and other Oriental languages, the philosophical sciences and all the branches of a common and liberal education, taught on an improved plan, in the most expeditious manner, in a way both scientific and applicable to practice in human life, etc."

One might say that after that *et* could only come a lot more *cetera*. However, certainly the most important one of the "additional unspecified persons or things" (that's what *cetera* means) necessary to education is *teachers*.

Why do people go into this often underpaid, sometimes maligned profession? Here's one explanation.

177. A teacher, Addie Wang, gave up a lucrative law practice to go into teaching. She says that people exclaim, "Oh, you're the one who was a lawyer and gave it up to teach first grade!" Then they ask, "Why did you do it?"

She replied that as a teacher she's helping the world, but had her doubts when practicing law. "There is no more drudgery and repetition than there was in the law, and teaching a lesson requires constant observation and adaptation, endless creativity and flexibility. Watching the flash of understanding on a child's face is as elating a feeling as any I have experienced."

She continues: "Children . . . are fresh and direct and eager, warm and funny, and many other things too rarely encountered in the . . . law. When a lawyer recently asked me, 'But don't you get tired of their childish ways?' I replied, 'At least they have the excuse of being children.' "

Teaching is rewarding, yes, but it's also a tough job because the world is changing and we teachers must use brains and care to avoid the "hardening of the categories" mentioned earlier.

178. At a large meeting of the Association for Childhood Education, which I attended in 1947, the world-famous anthropologist Margaret Mead (1901–1978) said this to the teachers: "There are only two kinds of teachers in the world today."

Here Mead paused, and the audience was rapt.

Mead continued, "There are those who learn everything all over again every five years; and there are those who say, 'The children are getting worse and worse.' "

But it's a relief now and then to suggest, without really meaning it, that the children *are* getting worse and worse, at least in some ways.

179. Mr. Price, high-school history teacher, was busy with his class on a spring day. It was hot, so the windows were open. Just outside some younger children were playing, and shouting—and disturbing the class. Mr. Price stuck his head out the window and yelled at the noisiest youngster, "Hey, young man, how old are you?"

"I'm eight years old," replied the kid.

"Impossible!" replied Mr. Price. "No one could get that dirty in eight years."

Another kind of relief can come when teachers are relaxing at the end of the day in the faculty room.

180. One thing teachers need, especially at the end of a rainy Friday, is a place where they can relax and express their frustrations. It's a part of mental health. A good example follows. In the faculty lounge of an excellent elementary school, some teachers were talking about reincarnation. One teacher remarked "If there's anything to the idea of reincarnation, I know what I'd like to come back as."

"Oh, tell us what," said a couple of colleagues.

"I'd like to come back," said the teacher, "as a childhood disease."

It might have been the same afternoon when a teacher said, as they were discussing one child's problems, "His I.Q. is about equal to his temperature—when he's normal."

And speaking of I.Q. scores, how about this comment on marks?

181. A high-school student came home from school seeming rather depressed.

"What's the matter, son," asked his mother.

"Aw, gee," said the boy, "it's my marks. They're all wet."

"What do you mean 'all wet'?"

"I mean," he replied, "below C-level."

Now back to the classroom.

182. In art class the children were working with plasticine, a claylike substance that can be used over and over because it does not harden. A girl had made a very nice model of a creature with wings. She held it up and said to everyone, "See the angel!" There were exclamations of delight from the class and teacher. Then the girl quickly molded the angel back into a ball and asked everyone, "Okay, now. What's this?" Nobody could answer—except "a ball?"

"Nope," said the girl, "it's a hiding angel."

The next day when the children came into art class, they were accompanied by a visitor. Another child pointed at the ball of plasticine and said to the visitor, "You know what that is? It's a hiding angel."

If only we grownups could become as skilled as children in seeing the "hiding angels" in life.

One habit teachers must try very hard to avoid is *sarcasm*, because it can hurt, even though it's sometimes humorous. Here's an example.

183. The teacher called on Milton, who was looking out the window and didn't respond at all. So the teacher said, quite loudly and sharply, "Milton, what is your opinion of the question we're discussing?"

"Oh, I'm sorry, sir, I didn't hear you," said Milton. "I was lost in thought."

"Well," said the teacher, "I'm not surprised you were lost. I realize it's unfamiliar territory."

Some children don't pay attention on purpose. How about this wise kid?

184. A fifth-grade class was on an educational trip. As they rode along in the school bus, the teacher noticed that one boy was lying face-down in the aisle of the bus with his hands over his eyes. "What are you doing?" scolded the teacher. "Why are you lying in the aisle like that?"

"Well," said the boy, "if you don't see anything, you don't have to write anything."

We teachers have to admit that sometimes we are unconsciously narrow and have the idea that all the world's truth—at least in our subject—is contained in *our* head. Maybe that's what caused some fresh kid to define a teacher as "a creature where everything goes in the ears and out the mouth." We should become accustomed to—delighted by—the fact that there's sometimes more truth in that classroom of ours than we are aware of.

185. This story is humorous in a way, but it has a sad ending. The teacher of a third grade asked her class during arithmetic class, "What numbers between 1 and 10 can be divided by 2?"

A girl raised her hand eagerly and was called on. "Seven!" she replied smiling.

The teacher frowned. "Sally, *how* can seven be divided by two?"

"That's easy," replied Sally. "Three and a half and three and a half."

The teacher frowned even more. "All right, Sally, if you're going to be smart, you can leave the room.

Back to a more cheerful note: the practicality of children, even grammatical practicality.

186. A rather strict English teacher also had the responsibility of teaching "homemaking," as home economics used to be called. The teacher noticed a rather attractive student carefully applying lipstick and powder, rather than doing her home ec lesson.

"Janey," said the teacher, "you pay more attention to your makeup than you do to your homemaking lessons."

"Well," said Janey, "before I can homemake, I have to catch someone with whom."

Janey recognized that education reaches outside the classroom. And sometimes the "classroom" can be outdoors, as is the case with a Summer Nature Program that my wife helps organize and support in the Awbury Arboretum just outside the study-in-the-woods where I am writing this book. Here are two charming events that took place in the Awbury classroom.

187. The nature-study teacher was taking a small group of urban children around Awbury Arboretum in the middle of a crowded urban area in Germantown, Philadelphia. The group stopped beside a woodpile, and the teacher moved a log and held up a large slug for the children to see. Several of them touched the slimy creature and exclaimed, "Ugh!"

The teacher said, "That's all right. You can wipe your hands on my pants. I take them home every night and wash them."

One wide-eyed boy heard only part of the sentence and said, "You mean you take these insects home every night and wash them?"

188. In the Awbury Arboretum Nature Program, the teacher was introducing a unit on "The Five Senses." The dialogue with the teacher and the three-to-four-year-olds went thus:

Teacher: We have eyes for . . . ?
Children: Seeing!
Teacher: And a nose for . . . ?
Children: Smelling!
Teacher: And ears for . . . ?
One Child: Earrings!

Back to the indoor classroom. One of the classic excuses of students who haven't got their assignment ready is, "The dog ate my homework." But today that's rather old-fashioned.

189. A fifth grader looked downcast, so her teacher asked, "What's the problem, Carol? I hope it's not homework again."

"Well, uh, yes, it is," replied Carol. "I was stupid and made my homework paper into a paper airplane."

"Carol, you're right, that wasn't a very bright thing to do," said the teacher, "but this once I'll let you just unfold the paper and hand it in."

"Oh, but that won't work," said Carol, looking even sadder. "You see, the plane was hijacked."

One of the challenges of teaching is the ingenuity of students, even in the lower elementary school. If you'd been the teacher, how would you have responded to this event?

190. On the floor of the corridor just outside the second-grade classroom the teacher saw a pool of water. She reported it to the children and gave them a brief lecture on tidiness, good habits, health, and responsibility. Then she asked, "What nice child will volunteer to wipe up the mess?"

No answer; complete silence.

Then the teacher had an idea. "All right," she said. "Let's try something. We'll all put our heads down and cover our eyes, including me. Then perhaps the person who is responsible for the puddle will be kind enough to clean up the hall."

The children seemed to agree, and all heads went down, all eyes were covered. Soon there was a patter of little feet going out into the hall. There were sounds of busy activity with a bucket and mop and drips of water, and then things being put away. Then the patter of little feet back into the room—and silence.

"All right," said the teacher. "Fine! Now let's all look out in the hall and see what a good job has been done."

The class all crowded to the door and looked out. There in the hall, right next to the first pool was a second. Beside it was a large sign reading, "The Phantom strikes again!"

A part of school and college is marks, above or below C-level. For years I've said that any piece of written work should be given at least three marks, one for content (the most important), one for spelling (the least important, for most misspellings are phonetically logical and spelling has no correlation with intelligence), and one for mechanics (punctuation, capitalization, etc.). And marks should be A, B, C, D, or NC (no credit), not based on a scale of 1 to 100.

191. Some schools and universities go to ridiculous lengths to calculate the marks of students to the nearest point on a scale of 1 to 100, or even to the nearest tenth of a point. How can anyone, how *should* anyone, think that a student's ability in a subject can be so closely quantified, especially when one considers the vast number of abilities and performances that must be combined in a mark? How much sense does it make to give a student a mark of 83.5? About as much as this sign at the entrance to the apocryphal village of Jenksville:

> YOU ARE ENTERING JENKSVILLE
> Altitude: 1,580
> Population: 3,775
> Founded: 1837
> Total: 7,192

A problem many schools have is to motivate students to learn material for which there is apparently no use in real life. Well, here's a device which, as far as I know, no one has tried.

192. A mathematics teacher came into the faculty room after she'd been watching a basketball game. Her face was glowing. "I've got the greatest idea for teaching!" she exclaimed.

"What do you mean? What's the idea?" asked a couple of colleagues.

"Well, you know how hard it is for us to really teach fractions? The kids just don't seem to be motivated to learn them," she said.

"Yes, it's true," said a fellow math teacher. "So?"

"Well, the solution is to change the system of scoring in basketball. A free throw, $1\frac{1}{16}$ point; a field goal, $2\frac{3}{8}$ points; and a long-distance basket, $3\frac{1}{15}$!"

Here's another device for motivating students to do and behave well.

193. An elementary school teacher, well versed in educational jargon, asked for a small allotment of money for "behavior modification reinforcers."

Her superior saw the item and asked, "What in heaven's name is that?"

"Lollipops," the teacher explained.

Even more basic to good behavior and work than lollipops is this: Students should feel cared for and respected, even when their work is poor.

194. Talking computers were just coming into fashion in some schools, as was the idea that children should be respected for themselves, even though they made mistakes in their schoolwork. Young Bert was pushing the keys and getting his answers displayed on the screen. At one point the computer was heard to say, "Incorrect. Try again. But remember, just because I said you were wrong doesn't mean I don't love you."

Many of the best school teachers allow their students to think and talk together when a really interesting question or problem comes up. The effectiveness of this strategy is illustrated by this story about Abraham Lincoln, who, I think, would have been an excellent teacher.

195. In 1832, during the Black Hawk war (a conflict between the U.S. and the Sac and Fox Indians), Abraham Lincoln (1809–1865), then a young captain of the Bucktail Rangers, was in command of his platoon as they marched across the country. Lincoln was rather ignorant of matters of drill, tactics, and formations; and when his soldiers came to a fence and a gate, he had no idea how to deal with the situation in the proper military way. So he commanded, "Halt! Company dismissed for two minutes. At the end of that time, reassemble on the other side of the fence."

Quite different from this technique, I think, is the practice of a certain Miss Woodstock, a classic old-fashioned, no-nonsense teacher.

196. A fine independent school near Philadelphia is the Shipley School. On its seventy-fifth anniversary in 1970, a history of the school was published, *Courage for the Deed, Grace for the Doing*, by Frances Stokes Hoekstra. This delightful book calls students of many years ago "the drones in the beehive of Shipley." It quotes a speech by Isota Tucker Epes, once a student at Shipley, eventually its head. The speech was made in 1967 and describes a teacher's class in 1934–36:

"Miss Woodstock . . . packed our minds so tight with essay answers that when at last we sat down for the examinations in the late June humidity in the study hall . . . , our brains simply boiled over onto the paper like uncapped bottles of overheated soda pop."

Thus we get close to the subject of discipline in schools. The most common complaint parents make about schools, of course, is "lack of discipline." Unfortunately, they often seem to mean simple obedience: Students should stay out of trouble and ask no difficult questions. No matter what you might think about school discipline, you must concede that it requires subtle judgment on the part of teachers.

197. An experienced teacher, much loved and respected, managed to get the very best from her students. Someone asked her for the secret of her success. "It's a matter of careful judgment," she replied. "For example, usually what a youngster needs most is a pat on the back. Sometimes he needs it a little harder and a little lower."

I personally don't believe in corporal punishment as a form of discipline. (Once, though, when I was talking with a stubborn, bright seventh grader who refused to work or to explain why he refused, I was reduced to picking up a 595-page anthology textbook and hitting him on the head with it. It didn't do his head or the textbook any harm, but it made me feel better, and I think the shock effect improved his work.) In a survey I made of several hundred junior high school students a few years ago for my book *How to Live through Junior High School*, I found that a surprisingly large number indicated that they preferred a spanking to "a friendly talk with the teacher." But sometimes teachers are asked to make unfair judgments about when and whom to spank.

198. At a parent-teacher conference, a mother told the teacher, "My son Paul is a very sensitive boy."

"Yes," said the teacher, "I've noticed that. Is there anything we should do about it?"

"Well," said the mother, "if Paul misbehaves, please spank the boy next to him."

Naughty children aren't always bad, sensitive or not. Here's a true story.

199. A beautiful young child in fifth grade kept doing mischievous, naughty things in class, in the halls, and out on the playground. Sometimes she was caught, sometimes not. But finally the time came when she'd been caught so much that she was sent to the principal. She sat there and smiled at him as he recited her misdeeds. Then he asked, "Sandra, why do you behave this way?"

Sandra replied, "I like to take the risk."

Sometimes children apply discipline in their own ways. Do you think this one was effective?

200. It was Kindness to Animals Week at school, and a fourth grader came home full of pride. His parents asked him why he was so happy, and he told them that

each student had to do something special for the week
and that what he did had really worked.

"And what did you do?" asked the mother.

"I kicked a boy for kicking his dog."

No matter what you may think about discipline, I'm
sure that some sort of order is always better than chaos
(except for the two-minute period of near-chaos permitted by Abraham Lincoln).

201. A seventh-grade boy at Germantown Friends
School, Philadelphia, tended to be very mischievous.
One day he had been sent out of the room for five
minutes, but he decided to sneak away down the hall.
Just at that moment, the dean of the upper school saw
him and called out, "Hal, stop, I want to speak to
you!"

Hal didn't stop but ran farther down the hall and
turned into a large study hall filled with quietly working students. The dean came right into the room and
grabbed Hal firmly by the arm. Hal shouted, "Help!
Help! Reality's got me by the arm!"

Grammar and development of vocabulary are two elements of education, for better or worse. If you enjoy
fresh kids (not rude or impudent ones) you'll appreciate
the next two stories.

202. The teacher asked her vocabulary-development
class, "What's the difference between ignorance and
apathy?"

A rather fresh kid immediately raised his hand and
said, "I don't know, and I don't care."

And it may have been in the same classroom, now

dealing with grammar, where the teacher asked, "Give me two personal pronouns" and pointed to a certain child, who replied, "Who, me?"

203. In a grammer lesson in eighth grade Mrs. O'Neill said, "Paul, give me a sentence with a direct object."

Paul replied, "Everyone thinks you are the best teacher in the school."

"Thank you, Paul," responded Mrs. O'Neill, "but what is the object?"

"To get the best mark possible," said Paul.

Up till now, we've been considering elementary-school education, not so-called "higher education." We need to be careful about that word "higher." The age of students is higher, but not the importance of what's learned. My experience has taught me perhaps first and second grades are of the highest importance, with grades seven and eight next. However, let's not argue about that. There's no doubt that Sir Isaac Newton (see story number 165) wouldn't have worried about it, nor would he have agreed with the teenager in this story.

204. A teenage girl was seated at dinner next to a very famous scientist, who had a long career of discovering new scientific principles. However, the girl did not know who he was and, to make conversation, she asked, "And what do you do, sir?"

"I'm studying science," replied the professor.

"You are? *Studying* science?" said the girl in amazement. "Why, I finished science at the end of tenth grade."

It is reliably reported that it was Derek Bok, President of Harvard, who said, "If you think education is expensive, try ignorance." My view, borne out by the experience of my own children and their spouses, is that you can get a good education in almost any college or university if you go after it. Consider this:

205. When Arnold Post, late professor of classics at Haverford College, heard that people were complaining about high tuition costs, he said, "Education is the one commodity of which people take a lot less than they pay for."

While we're on the subject of paying for education, enjoy this story from across the Atlantic.

206. Because of economic conditions, a famous English independent school (what used to be called a "public school") was obliged to raise its tuition. A letter informed parents of this fact stating that the increase would be £500 pounds *per annum*, except, unfortunately, it was spelled *per anum*. An angry parent wrote to the headmaster of the school thanking him for the notification and saying, "For my part I would prefer to continue paying through the nose, as usual."

Another aspect of higher education is experiments that push ahead to the frontiers of truth.

207. Martha Minow, a professor of law at Harvard, reported to her classes that scientists in their experiments were gradually switching from rats to lawyers, and she explained why: (1) There are more lawyers;

(2) Scientists tend to become emotionally attached to rats, which may tend to bias their conclusions; (3) There are some things rats just won't do.

So much, for the moment, for scientific experiments. Let's move on to literature, a broader (or narrower?) subject. We can also move from Harvard to Yale.

208. William Lyons Phelps (1865–1943), a professor of English at Yale, gave an examination on English literature just before Christmas. One student handed in a very short paper, reading, "God only knows the answer to this question. Merry Christmas!" Phelps returned the paper after Christmas vacation with this note: "God gets an A; you get an F. Happy New Year!"

As education gets "higher," the departments become more specialized and separated. When different "majors" come together in the same course, the results can be remarkable.

209. One liberal arts class was attended by majors in several different subjects. The professor began the first day with a "Good morning!"

A meteorology major looked out the window and thought, "It's true."

A psychology major pondered deeply, "Now what did he mean by that?"

An education major wrote it down.

When "majors" try to write doctoral dissertations, the results can be catastrophic—or universal.

210. There are those who think that studying for a Ph.D. degree, for which one must choose an exact thesis topic on which no one has written before, is bad for the mind, closing it to great and stimulating ideas. This phenomenon caused someone to say about a friend deep in her dissertation, "It seems to me that she's learning more and more about less and less, and I'm really afraid that by the time she has her degree she'll know everything about nothing."

Or the last line could be "nothing about everything."

211. Teachers, especially in "lower education," have vast power. Albert Shanker, head of the American Federation of Teachers, quotes this observation: "Teachers are the most powerful people in the world because who else can tell two hundred other people exactly when they can go to the toilet?"

This reminds me of the experience of E. M. Forster. You'll remember that he was the author of *Where Angels Fear to Tread*, *A Room with a View*, and *A Passage to India*.

212. E. M. Forster (1879–1970) had a very unhappy time in several rather foolish, cruel British boarding schools. In 1933, at age 54, he wrote this:

"If the impossible ever happens and I am asked to help break up a school [that is, take part in a school commencement], what I shall say is this: 'Ladies and gentlemen, boys. School was the unhappiest time of my life, and the worst trick it ever played me was to pretend that it was the world in miniature. For it hindered me from discovering how lovely and delightful and kind the world can be, and how much of it is intelligible. From this platform of middle age, this throne of experience, this altar of wisdom, this scaffold of character, this beacon of hope, this threshold of decay, my last words to you are, boys, there's a better time coming!' ''

We've thought about education at school and at university. Let's not forget about education at home. Here's an example of education at school spilling over into the home.

213. A young girl came home from school and was heard by her mother reciting her homework: ''Two plus two, the son of a bitch is four; four plus four, the son of a bitch is eight; eight plus eight, the son of a bitch—''

''Judy!'' shouted her mother. ''Watch your language! You're not allowed to use swear-words like *son of a bitch*.''

''But, Mom,'' replied Judy, ''that's what the teacher taught us, and she said to recite it out loud till we learned it all.''

Next day Judy's mother went to school with her daughter and right into the classroom to complain. ''Oh, heavens!'' said the teacher. ''That's not what I taught them. They're supposed to say, 'Two plus two, the sum of which is four.' ''

The teacher could have gone on to say, ''If you promise not to believe everything your child tells you about what goes on at school, we'll promise not to believe everything she tells us about what goes on at home.''

Here's another noble effort at direct education at home. Note the impeccable logic of the boy.

214. A father was trying to teach his young son the evils of alcohol. He put one worm in a glass of water and another worm in a glass of whiskey. The worm in the water lived, while the one in whiskey curled up and died.

"All right, son," asked the father, "what does that show you?"

"Well, Dad, it shows that if you drink alcohol, you will not have worms."

Another sort of home education is provided by correspondence courses. They can be very effective, but the effects are not always understood by close relatives.

215. A young man took a speed-reading correspondence course and was very pleased with the results. He wrote to his mother telling her how fast he could read and how much time it saved. His mother replied in a long letter, chatting about various events.

In the middle of her letter she wrote, "Now that you've taken that speed-reading course, I suppose you've probably already finished this letter."

Sometimes teachers can help parents deal with behavioral problems at home.

216. An eight-year-old boy had gotten into the very bad habit of swearing. He was scolded, punished, and pled with, but nothing could stop him. Finally, his parents asked his teacher for advice. "Well," she said, "why don't you try a positive approach instead of all these punishments? Find out what he really wants, and then tell him he can have it, but only if he stops swearing."

It sounded like a good idea, and the parents put it to the boy. He said that what he really wanted was a rabbit, and the parents gave him one on condition that he swear no more. And it was amazing. The boy stopped swearing completely, and he loved the rabbit so much he often carried it around the house.

Unbeknownst to the boy, the rabbit became pregnant. One evening, when there were guests to dinner, the boy carried the rabbit into the dining room just as it began to give birth to baby rabbits. He looked at it in amazement and horror and shouted, ''Christ! Hell! The damned thing's falling apart!''

''Damn!'' ''Christ!'' ''Hell!'' Perhaps we can use these concepts to lead us into the next chapter.

7

Religion

Religion humorous? Of course! Notice that this is the longest chapter in the book. For many people, religion is one of the deepest and most serious subjects of their lives . . . and afterlives. To say that it can't be humorous would therefore be irreligious, irreverent, and unfactual.

Since we ended the last chapter with some religious words used profanely, let's start this chapter on a modestly profane note.

217. A justice of the Supreme Court used to play golf at Chevy Chase with the Episcopal Bishop of Washington. One day, in a difficult situation, the Bishop missed the ball several times, but said nothing, only looked grim and disgusted. The judge looked at his friend and said, ''Bishop, that was the most profane silence I have ever witnessed.''

The next story is also about profanity and silence.

218. A moderately religious family owned, enjoyed, but was somewhat embarrassed by a parrot that swore a lot. They only truly minded it on Sundays. The parrot was trained not to talk when its cage was covered, so on Sundays they kept the cage covered all day long.

However, one Wednesday the family was surprised by an afternoon call from their pastor. Before they welcomed him into the parlor, one of the children rushed to put the cover on the cage. The pastor entered, and they all were enjoying tea . . . until there was a brief lull in the talk, when a voice was heard from under the covered cage: ''Damned short week!''

A parrot's profanity is rather superficial, I suppose, although the obvious question is: Where did it learn its vocabulary? Here are two more rather lighthearted profanity stories.

219. A sports fan was trying to persuade his churchgoing friend that baseball and football were really quite a lot like church.

''What do you mean?'' asked the church-goer.

''In church,'' said the fan, they say 'Stand up for Jesus!' At ballgames they say, 'For Christ's sake, sit down!' ''

220. At a well-known religious college, the academics were excellent but the food was utterly monotonous. Practically every dinner it was tomato soup, creamed chicken, mashed potatoes, string beans, and ice cream with chocolate sauce. One student who took his religion seriously, but who could hardly stand the food, said the same grace every evening at dinner. He quoted from *Hebrews*, 13:8: ''Jesus Christ, the same yesterday, and today, and forever.''

Profanity in the bleachers, profanity at the college dining room table—perhaps these can be expected. And we've already had a story about profanity on the golf course. But here's another golf-course story.

221. A businessman and a minister were playing golf together. The businessman kept missing the ball or driving it into the rough, and each time he did he snarled, "Oh, shit!"

After several "Oh shit!"'s, the minister said, "George, you mustn't use language like that. God will punish you."

But a few minutes later, the man's shot again went haywire, and he shouted, "Oh, shit!"

With that, a hand reached out of a cloud and thrust down a bolt of lightning, which hit the *minister*. And then a deep voice came out of the cloud: "Oh, shit!"

So God does send down punishment from Heaven, direct and harsh. However, not everyone believes it, at least not until there is very convincing evidence.

222. Robert, age eight, was the son of strict Presbyterian parents. He was very, very good, worked hard at school, did his chores, and was generally helpful and obedient. But one morning, for some reason, he came down to breakfast in a very nasty mood. When his mother served him prunes, he snarled, "I don't want prunes," and he refused to eat them.

His parents were aghast, and his father said, "Robert, you know that God commanded children to honor and obey their parents, and He will punish those who do not."

But Robert still refused and was angrily sent back to bed, and the prunes were put in the refrigerator.

A few minutes later, a terrible thunderstorm came up, with great roars and flashes of lightning. "Ah, wonderful," said Robert's mother, "this will teach him a lesson."

Robert came back down the stairs, went into the kitchen and opened the fridge. From there, just after another flash and roar, the boy's voice was heard saying, "Hell of a fuss to make about a few stupid prunes."

I am a Quaker; I know a lot of Jews. In fact, one of my sons-in-law is a Jew, as is my jogging companion with whom I've run more than 25,000 miles over the last twenty-one years. Do Quakers and Jews use profanity? Well, here's a mild case.

223. It's surprising how people tend to use sacred names in a very irreverent way. An example: Near the end of World War II, three Jews working for the Jewish Joint Distribution Committee, and a Quaker, working for the American Friends Service Committee, were riding in a jeep northward through Italy at a time of terrible bombing. They drove over the top of a steep slope, and there they saw that a beautiful cathedral had been totally destroyed. The three Jews, almost with one voice, exclaimed, "Jesus Christ!" while the Quaker exclaimed, "Holy Moses!"

Perhaps Jews and Quakers are less big on sin than other religious groups, but there's no doubt that there *is* sin in the world. Can any readers consider themselves innocent of at least one or two of the classical seven deadly sins?

(They are: pride, covetousness, lust, anger, gluttony, envy, and sloth.)

As you probably know, Catholics (and people of some other churches) are required to confess mortal sins, those committed deliberately and seriously. But even these confessions of sin can have their lighter moments.

224. A deaf old lady had a tendency to shout when she went to confession. When the priest asked her to speak more quietly, since everyone in the church could hear, she shouted, "What did you say?" So he carefully told her that she should write down what she had to say, in advance.

At her next confession, she knelt and handed a piece of paper to the priest. He looked at it and said, "What is this? It looks like a grocery list."

"Mother of God!" said the lady. "I must have left my sins at the A & P!"

225. In a large, empty, silent church, the priest was hearing confessions. At the back of the church the janitor was polishing brasses and replacing candles. He could hear everything that was being said.

A man came in and went into the confession booth and said, sadly, "Oh, Father, I have sinned three times." And then there was a mumbled recital of the sins. Then the priest said, "My son, your sins are forgiven. Now, if you'll just put $5 into the collection box, that will be fine."

Next was a woman. "Oh, Father, I have sinned three times"—and again the mumbled recital, forgiveness, and the priest saying, "Now if you'll just put $5 into the collection box, that will be fine."

Soon another man came in, "Oh, Father," he said

contritely, "I have sinned twice." Before he could go on, the janitor stated audibly from the back, "Go out and sin again, brother. Special today, three sins for $5."

Sinning can be enjoyable. If not, who would sin? Look again at that list of the seven deadlies! In the next story a woman admits such enjoyment, but perhaps a bit too late.

226. A pastor was discussing with an elderly church member a relative of hers who had seen the light and joined the church after a lifetime of riotous living. "Will my converted cousin's sins be forgiven, Pastor?" she asked.

"Oh, certainly, yes! Remember, the greater the sins, the greater the saint."

The woman thought silently for a time. Then she said, "Oh, Pastor, I wish I'd known this fifty years ago."

The woman above would have agreed with the world-renowned subject of the next story.

227. Heinrich Heine (1797–1856), a great German poet and supporter of revolutionary social ideals, was famous for his barbed wit. About religion, he wrote: "I love to sin. God loves to forgive sin. Really, this world is admirably arranged."

Another cynic, anonymous and probably not a poet, observed that the ideal life would be to go to church, be saved and destined for paradise, and then immediately be hit by a speeding truck after walking out the church door.

Probably the best-known story in the Bible about sin is the one about Jesus rescuing the prostitute from the condemning crowd (*John*, 8:1–11). Someone has retold the story in a totally *un*authorized version.

228. Some Scribes and Pharisees brought to Jesus a woman taken "in the very act" of adultery. They said that the law of Moses commanded that such a woman should be stoned. And they asked Jesus, "What sayest thou?"

Jesus wrote with his finger on the ground, thinking, and then stood up and said, "He that is without sin among you, let him cast the first stone."

At that, a large rock came down out of the clouds and killed the prostitute.

Jesus looked up toward Heaven and said, "Aw, Dad, I'm trying to make a point here!"

Just to be sure you have things straight, I remind you that in the actual Bible story all of those present, "convicted by their own conscience," went out one by one, leaving Jesus alone with the woman, to whom he said, "Hath no man condemned thee? . . . Neither do I . . . Go, and sin no more."

In this world we occasionally get a strong and direct invitation to go sinning.

229. There was a large revival meeting on the outskirts of town, and at the appropriate corner there was a large sign proclaiming: "If you're weary of sin and want to be saved, turn here, go 100 yards, and come into the revival tent."

Below the sign someone had hung another smaller one: "If *not* weary, call 876-3550."

Now to move to a more positive aspect of religion: *prayer*. We can pray for forgiveness, we can pray for what we want, we can pray for what the world needs. Many are the uses (and misuses) of prayer. The humorous stories I know about prayer mostly have to do with children.

230. A young girl, dressed in her Sunday best, was running as fast as she could to Sunday school. As she ran, she prayed, "Dear Lord, please don't let me be late! Dear Lord, please don't let me be late!"—at which moment she tripped on a curb and fell, getting her clothes dirty and tearing her dress.

She got up, brushed herself off, and started running again, praying, "Dear Lord, please don't let me be late! Dear Lord, please don't let me be late! . . . But *don't shove* me!"

Do children need guidance in the proper way to pray? I expect they do, but not always.

231. The mother of a religious family was listening to her daughter saying a rather lengthy bedtime prayer. "Dear God," prayed the child, "let me do well in my test tomorrow. Make my friends be nice to me. Tell my brother not to mess up my room. And please get my father to raise my allowance. And . . ."

The mother interrupted. "Don't bother to give God instructions. Just report for duty."

232. A small girl was reprimanded by her mother for laughing while saying her bedtime prayers.

"It's okay, Mom," she replied. "I was just sharing a joke with God."

And trust a kid to think up a fresh approach to prayer . . . and courage.

233. A British bishop was talking with a class of small boys and wanted to impress them with the importance of prayer and religious conviction. He said, "There was once a dormitory for seven boys. When lights-out time came, six boys stayed in bed, but one boy got out of bed, knelt down, and said his prayers. Now, boys, can you think of anything braver than that?"

"Oh, yes, sir," said a member of the class, "I can."

"You can?" said the Bishop, a bit taken aback. "Well, tell us about it."

"It's this way," the boy said. "There was a dormitory with seven bishops in it. When the lights went out, six bishops got out of bed, knelt down, and said their prayers, but one bishop stayed in bed."

Do animals pray? I doubt it, but who knows for certain?

234. Years ago, a missionary met a man-eating lion as he was walking from one village to another. The missionary fell to his knees and buried his face in his hands. Nothing seemed to be happening; the lion was silent. The missionary peeped through his fingers and saw the lion on its knees, its face buried in its paws. The missionary said in a trembling (but relieved) voice, "I'm praying to be delivered from the jaws of death. But what on earth are you doing?"

The lion growled, "I'm saying grace."

What did that lion believe? My guess is that he was "just going through the motions." And the missionary? Did he have faith? It seems that he probably didn't have enough. What *is* enough faith? The next story raises the question in an interesting way.

235. A very religious man, who had total faith in God, lived in a house by a great river. One night there was a terrible flood and the man had to climb up on the roof of his house to escape being drowned.

After a time some men came by in a boat to rescue him, but he refused. "I have faith that God will rescue me." Soon after, another boat came to rescue him, and again he refused: "I have faith in God." Considerably later a helicopter flew over and let down a rope ladder, but the man waved them away, shouting, "I have faith in God to rescue me!"

At last, the force of the water broke up the house and the man was drowned. He went to Heaven, and when he saw God he asked, "Oh God, God, I had such faith in you, and you let me drown. Why? Why?"

"What do you mean, let you drown? I sent you two boats and a helicopter, didn't I?"

So God performs his wonders in mysterious ways. And many preachers point out to their congregations that only if there is really deep, complete faith will prayers be answered.

236. In a rural, quite religious farm community, there was a disastrous drought and the crops were dying. In desperation, the local preacher announced that the whole community would assemble at the edge of one of the fields and pray for rain. A large crowd gathered, and the preacher climbed on a bale of hay and surveyed the flock. He said, "Brothers and sisters, you have come here to pray for rain."

"Amen!" responded the crowd.

"Well," said the preacher, "do you have sufficient faith?"

"Amen! Amen!" shouted the crowd.

"All right, all right," said the preacher, "but I have one question to ask you."

The crowd stood silent, puzzled, expectant.

"Brothers and sisters," shouted the preacher, "where are your umbrellas?"

Touché, preacher! No one can accuse the woman in the following story of having insufficient faith.

237. A very devout woman who just recently learned to drive a car always started her trip with a prayer: "Lord, guide my hands to steer this car." However, one day she found herself in a terrifying situation, with a car speeding up behind her, another passing just in front of her, and yet another coming rapidly at her from a road on the left. She did not know what to do, and so she threw her hands in the air and cried, "Lord, take the wheel!"

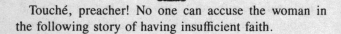

There is faith in God; there is faith in oneself. Which did the boy in the next story have?

238. In an elementary school art class, the children were being allowed to draw pictures of anything they wanted. A visitor was walking around the room and asked one boy, "What's that a picture of?"

"God," replied the boy.

"But," commented the visitor, "no one knows what God looks like."

"Well," the boy said, turning back to his work, "they will when I finish this picture."

Faith is *believing*—without evidence, if necessary. Can one have too much belief? What about this happy child?

239. It was "sharing time" in a kindergarten full of bright children. The teacher was presiding over a discussion about the children's fathers and mothers. One child said, "Well, my mother's a Catholic and my father's a Jew."

"Oh, wow!" said another. "So what do you believe?"

"I believe in *everything*!" said the first child.

"What do you mean, everything?" asked another child.

"Well, you know," said the first child, "Jesus Christ, Moses, Snow White, everything."

Sometimes, even at the point of death, the forms of faith and belief can be puzzling to people.

240. A Jew was crossing the street in front of a Catholic church. He was knocked down by a hit-and-run driver and lay nearly comatose. A priest ran out, knelt, and started to administer the last rites: "Do you believe in the Father, the Son, and the Holy Ghost?"

The Jew moaned, "Me dying and he asks me riddles."

But it's not only Jews—well, some Jews—who are puzzled at the end. Here's a story about the faith of a Catholic.

241. The priest was administering the last rites to a critically ill Irishman. Before anointing the man, the priest asked, "Do you renounce the world, the flesh, and the Devil?"

The Irishman replied: "I think in my condition this is no time to offend anyone."

The moment of impending death is indeed a test of faith. Could you meet the test?

242. A lone hiker, as night descended, fell over a cliff. Luckily, he managed to grab hold of a small sapling and stop his fall, but his feet were still hanging over the gulf, and nothing but blackness was below. He shouted, "Is anybody down there?"

"Yes," replied a great voice. "I am down here. Let yourself go. You can trust me. I am God."

There was a long silence, and then the hiker shouted, "Is anybody else down there?"

Some people consider faith impractical; others admire it; others read it amazingly into the events they see.

243. An old convent was at last renovated and modern plumbing put in. This meant that there was suddenly a large supply of chamber pots. The very efficient Mother Superior felt that perhaps she could get a little cash for them to help the work of the convent, so she called one of the nuns and told her to take the pots into town to see what money she could get for them.

The sister, dressed in her traditional robe and veil, set off in the old convent station wagon, but on the way to town it ran out of gas. Being a practical woman, the sister got out, picked up a chamber pot, and carried it down the road to the nearest filling station, where it was filled with gas.

She returned to the station wagon and began to pour the contents of the chamber pot into the gas tank. Just then a large truck rounded the bend and squealed to a stop. The driver looked out of the cab and shouted, "Sister, that's what I call faith!"

The most comforting sort of faith that many religious people have is in life-after-death. Others wonder whether it exists. And then, of course, there is Hell. Do we believe in eternal, burning damnation? What a terrible afterlife that would be! The irreverent Mark Twain, however, wasn't sure where he wanted to go. "Heaven for the climate," he said, "Hell for the company." So here's a story about Hell.

244. A man died after living an unrighteous life, and found himself in a line waiting to enter the gates of Hell. This didn't shock him very much. But he was surprised that, when his turn came to go in, the Devil asked him, "Smoking or nonsmoking?"

Back to the ideas of Mark Twain. The girl in the next story probably would agree with him.

245. A small girl was impressed by two things: how difficult it was not to tell a falsehood from time to time, and how many people were always telling her that it's a sin to tell a lie. So she decided to investigate, starting with her father. "Dad," she asked, "have you ever told a lie?"

Dad: "Well, it wouldn't be true to say I've never lied."

Girl: "How about Mom?"

Dad: "Well, yes, when she felt the truth would hurt, I guess she lied."

Girl: "How about Gramps?"

Dad: "I guess he's like the rest of us. If pressed he—"

Girl (interrupting): "Dad, you know, it must be terribly lonesome up in Heaven—with nobody there but God and George Washington."

There are people who do want to go to Heaven, no doubt about it, even sinners.

246. The great American actor W. C. Fields (1880–1946) was famous for his raspy voice, his bulbous nose, and the drunken, rascally characters he played. It is said that when he was on his death bed, a friend came to visit him and was astonished to find him reading the Bible. His friend asked, "Bill, what in the world are you doing reading the Bible?"

Field's reply was, "Looking for loopholes."

Yes, people want to go to Heaven, but a major question is *when*?

247. An enthusiastic preacher, wanting to be sure that all his flock would be saved, presented the glories of Heaven very vividly—all the pleasures of paradise. At last, reaching the climax, he asked, looking out over the congregation, "All right, brothers and sisters, how many of you want to go to Heaven? Raise your hands."

Every person in the church raised a hand—except one. The preacher smiled out over the group, and then, with an expression of shock and dismay, pointed directly at the sinner. "Oh, brother, don't you want to go to Heaven when you die?"

The sinner looked at him: "Oh, yes, Preacher, I do want to go to Heaven *when I die*. But I thought you were getting up a party to take off right now."

Even some of the most profound skeptics and atheists have their doubts.

248. H. L. Mencken (1880–1956), whose pungent, often cynical essays were collected in *Prejudices* (six volumes!), was at least an agnostic, probably an atheist. Once, when he was thinking about his own eventual death, he said, "If I die and find myself standing before a Pearly Gate and an old man in robes with a golden key, I'll go right up to him and say, 'My name is Henry L. Mencken, and I've made a terrible mistake!' "

Let's make this next story the last one about the afterlife. The point of view, you'll admit, is original.

249. Some people, when regarding the imperfect state of the world, cannot help but believe that there must be a heaven to which those who live good lives go. The English poet Rupert Brooke (1887–1915), a romantic patriot who died during World War I, wrote a verse affirming his belief, in a poem titled "Fish":

This can't be all, wise fish aver,

For how unpleasant if it were! . . .
Somewhere, beyond space and time,
Is wetter water, slimier slime. . . .

Some of us learned about religion by attending Sunday
School. But some amazing things are said in Sunday
School, to wit:

250. The assistant pastor of a fundamentalist Christian
church was teaching some children the Sunday School
lesson before the main service. He decided to enliven
things a bit by posing them a riddle: "What is it that
collects nuts for winter, climbs trees, and has a bushy
tail?"

An eager youngster waved her hand. The pastor called
on her. "Well," she said, "I know the answer's supposed
to be Jesus, but it sure sounds like a squirrel to me."

251. A Sunday School teacher, hard up for subjects to
talk about, was discussing with her class how Noah
might have spent his time on the ark. A girl volun-
teered, "Maybe he went fishing."

A boy countered, "With only two worms?"

252. Some Sunday School children were studying the
early life of Jesus and were asked to draw pictures of
their idea of his family's flight into Egypt. The teacher
was going around the room and saw that one boy had
drawn a picture of an airplane, and she noticed that it
had four people in it. She said to the small artist,
"That's interesting. I see you have Joseph, and Mary,
and that cute little person must be the baby Jesus. But
who's the fourth person?"

"Oh," said the boy, "that's Pontius the pilot."

253. A group of young children in a Quaker Sunday School were asked to discuss what God is like. What are His qualities? Several responses were given: He's loving; He's powerful; He's everywhere; He cares for you; He speaks to everyone in a still, small voice; He created the world; He protects people—and then one child said, ''He's jealous.''

The class was aghast. God—great, good God—jealous?

The teacher said, ''Well, let's see if we can find any evidence. Let's look in the Bible.''

''But where shall we look?'' asked several children.

''Try the Ten Commandments, the Book of Exodus, Chapter 20,'' the teacher suggested.

The children opened their Bibles, and after a few minutes, one raised his hand and was called on. ''Here it is! It says, 'Thou shalt not bow down thyself to them, nor serve them: for I the Lord thy God am a jealous God—' ''

At this point a voice from the back of the room shouted, ''Holy cow, He admits it!''

This one didn't take place in Sunday School but in an *ad hoc* session.

254. To understand this true story, you must know that in the Catholic Church bishops wear black cassocks (robes), cardinals wear scarlet or purple cassocks, and only the Pope wears a white cassock.

In Oxford, England, the regional assistant bishop met with a group of children in a small church, and he engaged them in friendly conversation. He decided to ask them a question to see how much they knew about

Catholic practices. "Children," he said, "if a man came into the room dressed like me, but all in white, who would it be?"

There was a long silence, and some squirming and embarrassment. Then a boy raised his hand. "Yes?" said the bishop.

"Oh, I know, sir," said the boy. "It'd be the school cook."

There's a lot to learn about religion, but some exceptional young people feel they already know enough.

255. At age ten Queen Elizabeth II (1926–   ) of England, was at Glamis Castle and received a visit by a preacher. When he was leaving, he promised to send "Lillibet" a book. The future queen replied, "Oh, thank you so much. But please let it be not about God. I know everything about Him."

Those of us who go to church are often inspired and improved by the service—but not always. As I have said before, I am a Friend (Quaker) and most Quaker Meetings are based on silence, with no program. They are, therefore, a risky business. Here are two examples:

256. Some years ago, in a Quaker Meeting in Germantown, Philadelphia, an ancient member had the habit of preaching too long, too loud, and too frequently. The elders of the Meeting tried to deal with him—but to no avail. Finally they agreed that if the Friend spoke again, they would firmly escort him from the Meeting, no matter what.

Sure enough, next Sunday the old Friend arose and started speaking in his usual way. The two assigned members walked up beside him, held him firmly by the elbows, and carried him out of the Meeting. As they did so, he shouted, "Our Lord and Savior Jesus Christ rode into Jerusalem on the back of one ass, and I am being carried out of Meeting on the arms of two."

And that wasn't the end of it. The next Sunday, the old Friend sneaked into the basement of the Meetinghouse, opened the furnace door, and preached into the furnace, so that his voice boomed out mysteriously from all the heating registers.

257. In the Society of Friends when someone is troubled by a weighty problem and wishes to have the Meeting consider it, he "lays a concern before the Meeting." Many years ago an odd but delightful Friend, William Bacon Evans, was preaching at a Meeting in rural New Jersey. It was a hot summer day, and next to the Meetinghouse was a chicken farm. As Bacon Evans was speaking, a hen appeared at the open door of the Meeting, clucking, and slowly walked down the center aisle, still clucking. Bit by bit, Bacon Evans noticed that members were paying more attention to the hen than to his words, so he stopped, put his hands on his hips, looked directly at the hen, and said, "And what hast thou to lay before the Meeting?"

Beyond the rather small Society of Friends, there are many other Christian denominations. Some are rather extreme, if also resourceful.

258. An old-fashioned, hell-and-damnation preacher was scolding his congregation for their terrible misdeeds. "Remember what it says in the Bible," he thundered. "Jesus told us that for those who do evil there shall be weeping and gnashing of teeth." (*Matthew*, 22.13) At this point the preacher saw a very old parishioner grinning up at him, unconcerned, toothless. He accepted the challenge and pointed at the grinning gums, "Don't worry, James Lippincott. Teeth will be provided!"

Here's another example of making the best of a bad thing in a religious service.

259. The famous evangelist Dwight Moody (1837–1899), founder of the Mt. Hermon School and the Moody Bible Institute, was about to start the final service in one of his campaigns when an usher handed him a large envelope. Moody assumed it was some sort of notice and held up his hand for silence. He opened the envelope and took out a sheet of paper. The word "fool" was written on it.

Moody looked at his attentive audience and said, "This is most unusual. I have just been handed a message which consists of but one word—the word 'fool.' I repeat this is most unusual. I have often heard of those who have written letters and forgotten to sign their names, but this is the first time I have ever heard of anyone who signed his name and forgot to write the letter."

There's no doubt, from what we know of history, that Jesus of Nazareth was a plain and voluntarily poor man. Sometimes we need to be reminded of this, even if only indirectly.

260. One Sunday, the minister looked out over his well-dressed, successful, and complacent congregation. Then he started his Prayer: "Oh, Lord, have mercy upon us, and justify to some extent the high esteem in which we hold ourselves."

Voluntary poverty is one thing; determined ignorance is another.

261. Melville W. Fuller (1833–1910), tenth chief justice of the Supreme Court was presiding at a church conference when a delegate began a tirade against education and universities: "I thank God I have never been corrupted by contact with any college!"

Fuller interrupted, "Do I understand that the speaker thanks God for his ignorance?"

The speaker replied, "Well, yes, if you want to put it that way."

"Then," said Fuller, "All I have to say is that you have a great deal to be thankful for."

The liturgy and well-known words of a church service can come to have deep, comforting meaning to those who participate in them. On the other hand, they can become meaningless or even distorted, especially by children.

262. Three small siblings had a pet sparrow, which, alas, died. The children were very sad, and they decided to give the dead bird a really good burial service. Their families were faithful members of the church, so the children had some ideas of how to go about it.

The first step was to dig the grave in a carefully chosen spot in a corner of the yard. Then they solemnly prepared for the actual interment. One child held the sparrow over the grave, and another recited, "In the name of the Father, and the Son, and in the hole he goes."

263. A sister and brother in a rather religious and patriotic family were playing together, and their words were overheard by their parents. The boy recited at the end of a mock church service, "In the name of the Father, the Son, and the Holy Ghost—"

The girl continued in a strong voice, "—and the Republic for which it stands."

It *is* interesting how religion gets divided up into different organizations and sets of beliefs. Fortunately, in our Republic we are free to believe what we will, or even to believe nothing. But this next story concerns two believers, a Catholic and a Jew.

264. Two good friends, John and Jacob, a Catholic and a Jew, enjoyed discussing their family activities with each other. One day John seemed very elated. The conversation went something like this:

John: Jacob, Jacob, I am so happy!

Jacob: Why? What has happened?

John: At last, after much study and work, my son Tom has been ordained a priest!

Jacob: A priest? So what else is new? That's nothing.

John: What!? A priest nothing! What do you want— that he should be made a bishop?

Jacob: Bishop? Why that's nothing.

John (growing angry): A bishop nothing? I suppose you think he should be a cardinal?

Jacob: Cardinal? There are lots of cardinals. Cardinal is nothing.

John: What!!?? The next thing you're going to tell me is Tom should be made the Pope, is that it?

Jacob: Pope? Pope is not so much.

John: My God, so you want that he should be Jesus Christ himself?

Jacob: Well, why not? One of our boys made it.

A good many people, being devoted to the beautiful language of the King James Bible, believe that God spoke in 1611 English. But there are exceptions.

265. An elderly woman told her friends that she had decided to take up the study of Hebrew. When they asked why she did this at such an advanced age, she explained, "I want to be able to speak to God in his own language."

Sometimes, when you are younger, speaking Hebrew is far beyond your realistic expectations, even if you are a Jew. A more realistic objective is to get a good education. But there can be barriers. . . .

266. A Jewish boy's family moved to a new community where the public schools weren't very good, so his parents decided to try to send him to a Catholic school. This meant he had to have a special interview with the Mother Superior in charge of the school. "Son," she said, "you do have a problem. But maybe we can solve it. I'll give you some material, you study it hard, and then I'll give you a test to see if we can admit you."

The boy read and studied. But just to make sure, he wrote the key points under his belt.

The day came for the test, and he entered the Mother Superior's office. The dialogue went like this:

Mother Superior: ''Where was our Savior born?''

Boy (peeking under his belt)*:* Bethlehem.

Mother Superior: What was his father's name?

Boy (peeking under his belt)*:* Joseph.

Mother Superior: What was his mother's name?

Boy (again the belt)*:* Mary.

Mother Superior (smiling)*:* Good! And what was our Savior's name?

Boy: Calvin Klein.

The problems interreligious and interdenominational relationships can cause are not limited to the world of education.

267. Katherine, a young Catholic woman, fell in love with Orville, who returned her love. But this match was apparently not made in heaven, for, as Katherine explained to her mother, ''Orville is a Baptist and he's opposed to the idea of marrying a Catholic.'' The young woman began to weep uncontrollably.

''Now wait, Kathy,'' said her mother. ''Why not try some real salesmanship? Tell him how wonderful our church is. We're the first Christian church. Or tell him of our great beliefs, our martyrs, our saints, the marvelous service the Church has done for the world, the marvelous cathedrals and chapels, the promise of salvation, and the wonderful comfort and inspiration given by our priests through their words and their listening to our confessions and forgiving us our sins. You know all this. Go out and sell Orville on the Church!''

Katherine dried her eyes and agreed to try. She had a number of dates with Orville and for a while was looking happier.

But one evening after a date her mother heard her sobbing again. "What's the matter, darling?" asked Kathy's mother. "Didn't it work?"

"No, Mother, no!" sobbed Katherine. "I *oversold* him. He wants to become a priest."

But back to Quakers again. They sometimes feel a "concern" to visit other religious groups who have compatible ideals ("testimonies") and need encouragement.

268. There is a small religious sect, the Dukhobors, many of whom moved from Russia to Canada around 1900 and settled near Vancouver. Somewhat like Quakers, they preached equality, pacifism, and total openness. Unlike the Quakers, however, they totally undress themselves and lie on the ground, open to God as a part of their religious exercise.

In the 1950s, there was "concern" among Quakers in Philadelphia that an important Friend visit the Dukhobors and assure them of fellowship and support. A wonderful member of the Philadelphia Yearly Meeting, Anna Cox Brinton, was appointed to go. She had a fine experience with them. When the time came to undress, Anna Brinton, a woman of courage, undressed with all of them and lay nude on the river bank.

Later, when she was telling about the experience, a fellow Quaker asked, "Well, Anna, how did thee feel, there on the bank?"

Anna replied, "I felt quite comfortable, but I kept asking myself, 'What would Friends in Philadelphia think?' "

Some Friends have also had contact with Black Muslims, and one told me this story.

269. A member of the American Muslim Mission, popularly known as the Black Muslims, was brought to court for a crime of conscience. He was alone, and the judge asked, "Where is your lawyer?"

"Allah is my counsel," the accused replied.

"Yes, I understand," said the judge, "but does he have a local representative?"

A member of my Quaker Meeting in Germantown became very much attracted to the Catholic Church, its firm and definite beliefs, and the excellent work it was doing in the community, especially among the poor. He felt that he could carry out Quaker social testimonies better as a part of that church, and he became a Catholic, but without dropping his Quaker membership. He's now a Catholic Quaker, or a Quaker Catholic! When he learned that I was collecting humorous stories, he would tell me stories about Catholics. Here are three:

270. This took place in a monastery where the monks had taken vows of silence. They were allowed to speak only once a year. One year, Brother Anselmo said, "A man just rode by on a brown horse."

A year passed, and Brother Joseph said, "It wasn't a brown horse; it was a gray horse."

At the end of the third year, Brothers Anselmo and Joseph were surprised to see Brother Elias descending the monastery stairs carrying a suitcase. Their quizzical looks elicited this comment, "If you fellows are going to argue all the time, I'm leaving."

271. In an enclosed convent, the novices had taken vows of silence. The rule was that they were allowed to speak two syllables per year to the Mother Superior, and that was all. After her first year, a novice had her session with the Superior, "Well, sister," asked the Superior, "what would you like to say? Remember, only two syllables."

"Beds hard," said the novice.

"But they're clean and good for the back, I think you'll find. I'm sorry you feel as you do. God bless you, sister."

At the end of the second year, the novice was again asked what she would like to say.

"Food stinks," she replied.

"But, sister," said the Superior, "it's made of the best whole-ground wheat, and the water is natural spring water, very good for the health. God bless you."

And so the third year came around, and this time the novice was carrying her possessions in a small sack. "Well, sister, what have you to say this year?"

"I quit."

272. There are a number of holy orders in the Catholic Church, among them the Benedictines, the Dominicans, and the Jesuits—also known as the Society of Jesus, or "S.J." Recently there was a dispute—quite possibly foolish—between some Benedictines and Dominicans as to which order was loved the most by God. After an examination of history, personal experience, and resort to prayer, no agreement could be reached. So the monks decided to send an angel messenger up to God Himself to ask the question.

After a few days the angel returned bearing a mes-

sage: "I bless both the Benedictines and the Dominicans and envelop you all in my love." The message
was signed, "God, S.J."

An editor passed this Catholic tidbit on to me.

273. A publisher received the following letter from a
monastery:

Dear Friends:

I ordered paperback #509, *The Adventures of Father
Brown*. You sent me #510, *Is Sex Necessary?* As we
here are committed to a negative answer, I am returning the book.

One of my own fervent beliefs about religion is this:
Unless it helps us make a better world right now, we'd
better look for other forces. I agree with William Penn
(1644–1718) who wrote: "True Godliness does not turn
men [and women] out of the world but enables them to
live better in it and excites their endeavors to mend it."
Note the verb *excites*. So, let's look at some stories that
show how religion and religious people apply (or fail to
apply) their religion to life at home and in the community. We might as well start with a Marx brother, to give
perspective.

274. Groucho Marx (1895–1977) was famous (along
with his brothers Harpo and Chico) for his slapstick
comedy, outrageous puns, and wisecracks. One day,
when he was getting out of an elevator, he happened
to meet a priest, who came up to him and put out his
hand, saying "I want to thank you for all the joy you've
put in the world."

Groucho shook hands and replied, "Thank you, Father. And I want to thank you for all the joy you've taken out of it.''

I think, by the way, that it was Groucho who said to his brother, who was squirting water on the crotch of his trousers, ''What are you trying to do—make it look like an inside job?'' But that's not religious.

One of the ways to support the activities of the church, and also to be useful in the world, is to provide a needed service.

275. The church choir was putting on a car wash to raise money to pay their expenses for a special trip. They made a large sign, CAR WASH FOR CHOIR TRIP, and on the given Saturday business was very good. But by two o'clock the skies clouded and the rain poured and there were hardly any customers. Finally, one of the girl washers had an idea. She printed a very large poster which said, WE WASH [then an arrow pointing skyward] GOD RINSES.

Business boomed!

We've given examples of prayer, but not of how painful really religious people can be.

276. A small girl was kneeling at her bedside, saying her prayers, her mother listening and waiting to kiss her goodnight. She heard the girl say, ''Oh, God, make the bad people good, and the good people nice.'' This girl's observation recalls an ancient aunt of mine, very religious and very humorous, who used to say, ''A martyr is someone who has to live with a saint.'' (It works the other way round, too.)

The late Cardinal Cushing of Boston would agree. He said, "Saints are okay in Heaven, but they're Hell on earth." Holiness, if tainted with self-righteousness, can weaken the mind. For example:

277. Nicholas Brown (1729–1791) was asked why he had given money to found Rhode Island College, later named Brown University. He replied: "My Baptist faith had done so much to vulgarize the American mind that I felt obliged to make some recompense."

I think our old friend Mark Twain would have approved of Nicholas Brown.

278. An unprincipled businessman, who liked to appear full of virtue, told Mark Twain (1835–1910), "Before I die, I'm going to make a pilgrimage to the Holy Land. I shall climb to the top of Mount Sinai and read the Ten Commandments aloud."

"I have a better idea," said Mark Twain.

"You do?" said the businessman. "I'd like to hear it."

"About the Ten Commandments," Twain replied, "why don't you stay right at home in Boston and *keep* them."

Twain would also have appreciated this next story. It happened a long time ago.

279. In a small town in medieval Europe a poor peasant earned his living by carting loads of goods for people. But after many years, his old horse died, and the peasant was in despair. He went to his priest, who said, "Never mind, all will be well. Just come with me."

"Oh, can it be so easy?" asked the peasant.

"Yes," said the priest, "just come up the hill with me."

So they walked up to the hill to the baron's estate and right into his magnificent stables. There was a splendid array of horses. The priest said, "Take your pick."

"What?" said the peasant, "That would be stealing from the baron!"

"Never mind, everything will be all right. Take your pick."

So the peasant chose a splendid draft horse and led it down the hill. The priest, meanwhile, went into the horse's stall and fell fast asleep.

An hour or so later, the baron came to the estate and decided to look over his horses. He was amazed to see the priest sleeping on the straw in one of the stalls. "Father! Father!" he said, waking the priest up. "What are you doing sleeping in my horse's stall?"

The priest looked bewildered, and then sat up, exclaiming, "A miracle! I must have been forgiven!"

"What do you mean?" said the baron.

"I will explain," said the priest. "When I was a young priest, I used to hear the confessions of a very attractive young woman, and, well, one thing led to another and, we, uh, well, you know what happened."

"Yes, yes," said the baron, "but why are you sleeping in my horse's stall?"

"Because God punished me," said the priest, "and reincarnated me as a horse, a beast of burden. But now, here I am a man again! Oh, what a miracle! God is good!"

The baron was amazed and bade farewell to the

priest, who walked down the hill with a glad expression on his face.

Meanwhile, the poor peasant was happy, doing well with his splendid new beast. One morning, a week later, the baron came down into town and saw the peasant carting a load. The horse somehow looked familiar. The baron stopped the peasant, who was now trembling. He saw his own brand on the horse. He examined the horse's teeth. Yes, there was no doubt, it was his horse.

The baron backed off a bit, looked severely at the animal, and said, "Well, Father, I see you've been at it again."

And speaking of theft for "holy" purposes. . . .

280. Desmond Tutu is the Anglican bishop of Johannesburg, South Africa. With a smile and some sly wit, he is able to make important points with a minimum of bitterness, which is perhaps why he was awarded the 1984 Nobel Peace Prize. He demonstrated this skill in a recent speech in New York City, where he stated, "When the missionaries first came to Africa, they had the Bible and we had the land. They said, 'Let us pray.' We closed our eyes. When we opened them, the tables had been turned: We had the Bible and they had the land."

It is very difficult—in South Africa or anywhere—to see things from another's point of view.

281. As an act of Christian charity, a local bishop decided to have tea with a family in one of his parishes. On the appointed afternoon, he was formally greeted and shown into the parlor, where a beautiful tea had been set up. The bishop looked around, smiled at the hostess, and said, "I'm glad to see you are living so comfortably."

A young daughter of the house spoke up. "Oh, Bishop, if you want to know how we really live, you must come when you are not here."

282. A girl was going with her family through a large art museum. Toward the end of the visit, they came into a room full of religious pictures. One was a particularly gruesome painting of Christians being thrown to the lions. The little girl seemed to be fascinated by the painting. She stayed so long, and looked so intently, that her mother was concerned that she might be too deeply affected.

"Come on, dear," said the mother. "We really should move on."

But the girl looked very troubled. So the mother asked, "Dear, what's the matter?"

"Oh, look, Mommy," said the child, "there's a poor lion that hasn't got any Christian."

There may be a few lions in this world who haven't got any Christians—figuratively speaking. Similarly, there are jobs that must be done even when no one is willing to volunteer to do them. Even among Quakers this is true.

283. One of the most appealing bits of the Hebrew Scripture is found in the Book of *Isaiah*, Chapter 6, verse 8, when the prophet's sins are purged by an angel and then the Lord is heard saying, "Whom shall I send, and who will go for us?'' and Isaiah responds, ''I, here am I; send me.''

At a large Quaker meeting in the late 1940s, after the creation of the State of Israel, a respected, neutral person was needed to act as mayor of Jerusalem until things got stabilized. One of the best known figures among Quakers was Clarence Pickett, Executive Secretary of the American Friends Service Committee. He had had much experience as a peacemaker in tense situations. As the meeting proceeded, the question kept being raised, ''Who will go? Who will face the dangers of acting as mayor of Jerusalem?'' At last a weighty Friend arose and said in an impressive voice, ''Here am I. Send Clarence.''

Meanwhile, what is the person who proclaims, ''Here am I, send X,'' doing? Probably improving his or her own situation in the world.

284. A woman went into one of the largest bookstores on Fifth Avenue, in New York City, and asked a clerk to direct her to the section on Religion. ''I'm sorry,'' said the clerk, ''we no longer have a Religion section. What you want is either Nonfiction or Self-Improvement.''

Even members of the clergy need to improve themselves, some more than others. Such need may cause them to ignore urgent local situations in the parish. Consider this notice in a church bulletin.

285. *Absence.* I shall be away from the parish attending the Diocesan Clergy School from April 21–24. It will be convenient if parishioners will abstain from arranging to be buried, or from making other calls on me during this time.

We'll end this chapter on religion with another story about H. L. Mencken, who was about as unreligious (in a conventional sense) as you can become.

286. H. L. Mencken (1880–1956) enjoyed making fun of revered people of his day and in history, and in his mocking he often spoke much truth. He did not like the self-righteous Puritans, many of whom, cast out of the Church of England, migrated to America, where they endured many hardships and took a narrow, self-righteous view of life. This caused Mencken to define Puritanism as "the lurking, lingering fear that somewhere, someone may be happy."

8

Politics and Politicians

We need politicians to make policy, and they don't get all the credit they deserve. Our nation needs policies, and it needs politicians. But sometimes politicians are funny, intentionally or otherwise. Although this chapter is very short, it could have been much longer, since most of the stories in this book could be applied in one way or another to politicians. Try it and see. In fact, one of the tragedies of modern politics is that some sourpusses believe that funny politicians are not serious. Remember, humor is serious business—and so, politicians, be humorous! If you are, we readers *might* vote for you.

We'll start with the basics: before the beginning of the world.

287. A doctor, an engineer, and a politician were arguing about which profession came first. The doctor said, "Well, Eve was created out of Adam's rib. That was obviously surgery."

"Possibly," said the engineer, "but don't forget, the world was created out of chaos. That was certainly a job done by engineering."

"Hey, wait a minute!" said the politician. "The chaos. Who do you think was responsible for that?"

Any democracy is bound to contain a degree of chaos, including the chaos created by insoluble problems. Here's the way politicians in Ireland, a wonderfully poetic democracy, dealt with such a problem.

288. It is said that many years ago the council of a town in County Cork, Ireland, was having a lot of trouble with criminals, and their jail was overflowing. But the town also had a great shortage of funds. The council dealt with the problem by passing a three-part resolution:

(1) The city shall build a new jail.

(2) The jail shall be built out of materials in the old jail.

(3) The old jail shall be used until the new jail is completed.

Since such solutions might look good at the time they are devised but later turn out not to work, politicians must be quick on their political feet or they'll get blamed and kicked out of office. Was the stable hand in the next story training for a career in politics?

289. Some years ago, when mules were still widely used, a visitor to a stable watched a worker skillfully managing a rather lively mule. The visitor asked, "Does that mule ever kick you?"

"No, sir," the stable hand replied, "but he frequently kicks the place where I recently was."

Negotiation is a part of politics, and a part of negotiation is taking positions more extreme than the ones a politician will eventually settle for. If the press is present and reporting, it's vital to put up the appearance of a good fight, to express outrage, and to show your constituents that you're giving your all to the struggle for their interests. This is true in the politics of labor, too.

290. In England, a much more heavily unionized country than the United States, labor disputes are carefully reported in the press, and each side needs to be able to give the impression of doing its very best to win favorable terms. Recently, outside the negotiation room, the labor representative said to the representative of management, "I have an idea. Before we start negotiating, let's both practice walking out in disgust."

And there are international politics and power struggles, thank God! The alternative would be constant war. In the next story, both sides were serving their own side's interest while at the same time looking like considerate people.

291. When Chaim Weizmann (1874–1952), scientist, Zionist, and politician, became first president of Israel in 1948, an Arab sheik sent him a gift of a fine stallion. Weizmann ordered one of his aides to return the stallion.

"But, sir, it is a splendid gift," said the aide.

Weizmann replied, "A gift that eats is not a gift."

So, beware of gifts that eat. How about the Devil? Can he and his friends be useful?

292. A candidate for city council was doing some door-to-door campaigning, and things were going pretty well, he thought, till he came to the house of a grouchy-looking fellow. After the candidate's little speech, the fellow said, "Vote for *you*? Why I'd rather vote for the Devil!"

"I understand," said the candidate. "But in case your friend is not running, may I count on your support?"

This sort of good-humored wit can be useful, especially if the word gets around.

Yet another political skill is the need to make nice distinctions when judging what to do when people misbehave or seem hostile. This applies even to presidents.

293. All presidents of the United States have to endure a certain amount of abuse and ridicule. They must learn to put it into perspective. A fine example: William Howard Taft (1857–1930; president, 1909–1913) was dining at home and his youngest son made a disrespectful remark to him.

Mrs. Taft said, "Well, aren't you going to punish him?"

Taft replied, "If the remark was addressed to me as his father, he certainly will be punished. However, if he addressed it to the President of the United States, that is his constitutional privilege."

Insults and disrespect, I'm sure, occur more often outside than inside the home. With skill and a sense of humor, a politician can turn an insult into an advantage.

294. In 1858, Abraham Lincoln (1809–1865) was debating Stephen A. Douglas (1813–1861), his opponent in a campaign for the U.S. Senate. Not only was Lincoln not as great an orator as Douglas, he was also not what one would call a handsome man. At one point Douglas accused Lincoln of being two-faced. Lincoln replied, "I leave it to my audience. If I had two faces, would I be wearing this one?"

Some people think being tall is an advantage. Is it? Consider the following story about the son of a politician of sorts, Oliver Wendell Holmes, Jr. (1841–1935), for thirty years a U.S. Supreme Court Justice, know as the "Great Dissenter."

295. Oliver Wendell Holmes, Sr. (1809–1894), a physician, poet, and author (he wrote *The Autocrat of the Breakfast-Table*, a collection of essays) was a short man. Once he was at a gathering of unusually tall men, and he was asked by a friend whether he felt insignificant. "No, indeed," he retorted. "I feel like a dime among a collection of pennies."

And this brings us to the subject of insults, *carefully expressed* insults. Such expression is a political skill.

296. Alfred E. ("Al") Smith (1873–1944), a four-time governor of New York, was at a political meeting at which one of his opponents, said, "Come on, Al, and tell us all you know. It won't take long."

Smith replied, "I'll tell 'em all we *both* know; it won't take any longer."

297. After a long private meeting, two politicians came out to face some eager reporters. One reporter asked, "Was the meeting a success?"

"Yes," replied one of the politicians. "We had an excellent exchange of views."

"What do you mean, an exchange of views?" asked the reporter.

"Well, I'll explain," said the politician. "He came in with his views and went out with mine."

298. During the presidency of Calvin Coolidge (1872–1933; President, 1923–1929), a senator named George Moses complained to Coolidge that a man being considered for a Republican senatorial nomination was "an out-and-out S.O.B."

Coolidge replied, "That could be, but there's a lot of them in the country, and I think they're entitled to representation in the Senate."

Sometimes a politician can make some capital by insulting another state, although caution is needed here. Consider this anecdote about Arizona, the forty-eighth state, which entered the Union in 1912.

299. Many years ago, Senator Henry Fountain Ashurst (1874–1962) of Arizona said during his maiden speech in the Senate, "Mr. President, the baby state I represent has the greatest potential. This state could become a paradise. We need only two things—water and lots of good people."

Boies Penrose (1860–1921), a senior senator from Pennsylvania, begged to interrupt: "If the Senator will pardon me for saying so, that's all they need in Hell."

For such a genteel country, the United Kingdom's House of Commons is often the scene of an amazing amount of rude shouting, interrupting, and insulting—

more than would ever be tolerated in the House and Senate of the wild, youthful United States.

300. In the British House of Commons there is, or was, a very long urinal with a great row of appliances. One day, Clement Attlee (1883–1967), a leader of the Labour Party, was standing at a urinal near the door. Winston Churchill (1874–1965) entered and walked all the way to the other end of the room to urinate. Said Mr. Attlee, "Mr. Prime Minister, we're political opponents, but we don't need to be so distant to each other off the political floor."

Mr. Churchill replied, "Clement, the trouble with you is that whenever you see anything good you want to socialize it."

Most often, though, Englishmen—and members of the House—are able to get in their political puncturing more subtly.

301. A Texan was showing an English politician around the great state. At one point he commented, "Do you realize that your whole country could be fitted into one small corner of our state?"

"Oh, really?" said the Englishman. " 'Twould do wonders for the state, wouldn't it?"

In case you've forgotten, the area of the United Kingdom is 94,000 square miles and that of Texas, 267,000.

Let's leap across ocean and land and go to the Soviet Union, where I guess it's more dangerous to insult people, especially members of the secret police, the KGB, which is not exactly a tactful political organization. But somehow the following story got out and perhaps now is a part of *glasnost*.

302. It was 3 A.M. in Moscow, and Igor Abramovich was secretly studying the Bible in his apartment.

The door was suddenly kicked in, and some KGB men entered. "Why are you reading this book in Hebrew?" demanded the senior agent.

"Because when I die and go to Heaven I want to know how to speak the language," said Igor.

The agent smiled wickedly. "And what if you go to Hell?"

"I speak Russian already," Abramovich replied.

Now, back to the U.S.A., where swift and clever answers are coveted by politicians under stress.

303. An American congressman, asked a difficult question on a touchy subject, replied: "That's an excellent question. And all I can say is, where would this country be without this great land of ours?"

Perhaps the same politician, after the session, went to a bar and told the waiter: "Fix me a drink that reflects traditional American values."

As I suggested earlier, even justices of the Supreme Court have to be politicians to some extent. This is even more true of ordinary judges, most of whom are elected, not appointed, to their positions. It's nice, then, to find a few who keep their modesty and sense of perspective.

304. Judge Robert S. Gawthrop, who has held numerous high judicial posts, was first nominated and then elected to the bench in 1977 at the age of forty-four.

He once said, "Just because people stand up when you walk into court and you wear a black dress to work and sit on an elevated chair . . . , you have to remind yourself you're just another person who happens to be a lawyer elected to serve as a judge."

To make this clear to himself and to people who interview him, Gawthrop keeps a small framed statement near his private courtroom door—a gift from relatives: "To us you'll always be just the same old jackass."

To close this chapter, let's consider politicians from a totally different point of view.

305. Anita and Joan were discussing the condition of the world. Their friend Lorna was taking it all in.

Anita: What this world needs is more poetry and poets. We need their beautiful, inspiring ideas.

Joan: No, no. You've got it wrong. We've got to be practical. Poets just fly off into fantasy. Politicians aren't perfect, but they make the world work.

Anita: Well, maybe we could get the best of both worlds by encouraging politicians to write some poetry, and get some poets to go into politics.

Lorna (interrupting firmly): Well, I'll tell you one thing. The politics of poets shouldn't be taken any more seriously than the poetry of politicians.

So, politicians, stay away from poetry! To demonstrate how unreliable the opinions of poets are, I quote two bits from James Russell Lowell (1819–1891).

306. James Russell Lowell was professor of modern languages at Harvard and editor of the *Atlantic*

Monthly. Yet he wrote about politicians in his *Bigelow Papers:*

- "To the people they're ollers ez slick ez molasses, an' butter their bread on both sides with the Masses."
- "Skilled to pull wires, he baffles Nature's hope, who sure intended him to stretch a rope."

307. More sensible—and Lowell admits to being a satirist—is the comment Woodrow Wilson (1856–1924; president 1912–1921) made in a speech in St. Louis in 1919: "Things get very lonely in Washington sometimes. The real voice of the great people of America sometimes sounds faint and distant in that strange city. You hear politics until you wish that both parties were smothered in their own gas."

A humorous comment? Well, yes, if you remember that humor is the flip side of tragedy.

308. Let me quote Plutarch as a way of neutralizing the irreverence of this chapter. It's from the *Lives* of Plutarch (A.D. 46–120 [?]), the Greek essayist and biographer.

"The conduct of a wise politician is ever suited to the present posture of affairs. Often by forgoing a part he saves the whole, and by yielding in a small matter secures a greater."

9.

Speakers and Writers

Perhaps speakers and writers take themselves more seriously than most other groups, even though they sometimes hire "humor consultants." At least speakers have it easier than writers; they can always deny they ever said it, whereas a writer is down in indelible ink. Abolish tape recorders!

Some of the most humorous writing comes in short, delightful bits, as you will see. And note, if you are a speaker, that almost all of the stories in this chapter, not to mention this entire book, can be used in speeches. *However*, be sure that using the stories doesn't make your speeches longer! "Brevity is the soul of wit," says Shakespeare's Polonius (*Hamlet*, Act ii, scene 2).

309. One of society's problems, at least among those people who attend meetings, is that speakers don't stick to their time limit. Here are a verse and a song, both anonymous, that could help matters.

Time's Awastin'

I hold that speaker great
—A truly fine narrator—

Who says, "It's getting late,"
  And doesn't make it later;
Whose talk is no infusion
  Of long, trite platitudes,
And who says, "In conclusion,"
  And *concludes*.

An alternative way to surprise an audience: Stop your speech *before* they think it's going to end and sing the following to the tune of "*The Stars and Stripes Forever*:"

Be kind to your web-footed friends;
That duck may be somebody's mother.
Be kind to your friends in the swamp,
Where the weather is cold and damp.
You may think that this is the end.
Well, it is.

The virtue of brevity should be extended to the pulpit. Here's a practical suggestion.

310. A preacher tended to make his sermons much too long, and members of the congregation were looking for a way to tell him this in a tactful way. One Sunday, after the preacher came in with a bandaged finger, a parishioner asked him, "Pastor Smythe, what happened? How did you cut your finger?"

The pastor replied, "I was thinking about my sermon, and I cut my finger."

"Oh, I see," said the member. "Well, next time I suggest that you think about your finger and cut your sermon."

A related incident: A speaker told his audience, "I don't mind your looking at your watches to see what time it is, but when you hold them up to your ear to find if they are still going, that's too much."

Perhaps no speaking assignment is more tough than this one: a college president facing his faculty.

311. An irreverent professor was getting quite restless and bored as the new president addressed the faculty. When the president asked, "Are there any questions or comments?" The professor replied, "Mr. President, verbosity may be your long suit, but it's not long enough to cover your asinity."

How best to begin a speech can be a stimulating problem, but one must use one's sense of discretion or one can get into trouble—or give unintended laughs.

312. A politician who didn't speak well asked his friend for advice. His friend said, "You should start with a question—like, 'Why are we all here?' "

The politician tried out the idea before various audiences, and it went well—until he somehow got persuaded to speak to the inmates of an insane asylum. He began in his usual way, "Why are we all here?"

Quick as a flash came back a reply from a voice in the audience: "Because we aren't all there."

313. The governor of a state, wanting to demonstrate his concern for all parts of society, agreed to make a speech to the inmates of a prison. The appointed evening came, the audience was assembled, and the governor had his speech ready—except that he'd forgotten to figure out in advance how he would address the men. He was introduced, stood up, and began.

"Fellow citizens"—and there was a low laugh. The governor made another try: "Fellow convicts"—and there was a very loud laugh. So, finally he decided just to begin in his conventional way: "I'm glad to see so many of you here tonight."

Even before the speech begins, there is an introduction that is often wearisome, especially to the speaker. (I always tell organizers of meetings where I speak that I'll double my fee if the introduction lasts more than three minutes.) Sometimes introductions can be over-effusive.

314. A speaker had received an introduction that seemed to promise more than he felt he could deliver. He began his speech thus: "Once in Virginia, I passed a small church. In front was a large sign which read, ANNUAL STRAWBERRY FESTIVAL. In small letters below was printed, *On account of the Depression, prunes will be served.*"

We've heard from Abe Lincoln several times already in this book. He had a novel theory about the relationship among thinking, talking, and speech-making—at least in the case of his political opponent. Let's listen in on the great debater again:

315. Commenting on his bouts with Douglas, Lincoln said, "When I was a boy, I spent considerable time along the Sangamon River. An old steamboat plied on the river, the boiler of which was so small that when they blew the whistle, there wasn't enough steam to turn the paddle wheel. When the paddle wheel went around, they couldn't blow the whistle. My friend Douglas," said Lincoln, "reminds me of that old steamboat, for it is evident that when he talks he can't think and when he thinks he can't talk."

Most people will frankly admit that they felt great nervousness before making a speech.

316. A well-known British bishop once told his audience, "I feel rather like a swan."

The audience laughed, but was a bit puzzled.

The bishop continued, "I look all calm and serene on the surface, but I'm paddling like hell underneath."

Nervousness, then, is a problem no matter how well concealed. But there can be a worse problem, especially when alcohol is available.

317. A well-known professor was being honored at an open-bar reception, and he had had too much to drink. When he was introduced, he rose from his chair, staggered, and fell. The audience gasped. But the professor, as he lay on his back, said, clearly and cordially, "I think I shall dispense with my prepared remarks and simply take questions from the floor."

Alcohol can spoil "prepared remarks," but so can audience behavior.

318. Reinhold Niebuhr (1892–1971) was an American religious and social thinker, a political activist, and a very independent man. At one time he was asked to make a speech to the World Council of Churches, which asked him to write his speech out in advance so the august audience could be provided with copies.

As Niebuhr was delivering his speech, he became more and more annoyed that nobody was looking at him, and that just before he came to the bottom of each page, there was a loud rustle of papers. At last he stopped, waited until all eyes were riveted on him, tore up his manuscript, and threw the pieces at the audience. "Now," he said, "I defy you to follow me!"

Speeches can go badly for a lot of reasons—even sabotage. Consider the following dirty trick, which was almost pulled off.

319. A speech-writer for President Lyndon Johnson (1908–1973; president, 1963–1969) had been fired and was feeling angry. He knew Johnson usually didn't look at his cue cards before his speeches. Here are the cards the fired writer provided for Johnson's speech in hopes they'd be used and he'd get revenge.

CARD 1: "You have heard people say that we cannot fight a war half way around the world and still pursue the goals of our great society. Well, I say we can, and I will tell you how."

CARD 2: "You have heard people say that we cannot maintain an economy that makes jobs available to everyone and still win the fight against inflation. Well, I say we can, and I will tell you how."

CARD 3: "They say we cannot bring racial justice to America without anger and dissension. Well, I say we can, and I will tell you how."

LAST CARD: "O.K., Lyndon, you're on your own."

I find this story very useful to dramatize how important it is for people—like boards and executives, principals and faculties, parents and teachers—not to surprise each other by failing to communicate.

So much for stories about speakers. Now let's turn to some about writers, who also deal in words. I think most people who don't write professionally fail to recognize what hard work writing is. Well, reader, get some insight from this young schoolchild.

320. A third grader was struggling over writing a short story assignment in class. "Boy," she moaned, "I never realized Shakespeare had it so rough!"

It's less "rough" to write to a pen pal who lives in a foreign land. Fortunately for the cause of unintentional humor, one teacher took a few notes on these letters before they were mailed.

321. A class was assigned to explain the American monetary system to a pen pal. Here are some choice passages:

• "The money in our country is very easy to find what to do with it."

• "In coins we have pennies which are about the size of a small circle."

• "In US money we use the dismal system."

• "With a quarter you can buy toys, fake fingernails, and other things."

• "I'm sorta kinda scatterbrained and therefore know very little about money."

• ''About the names we use, some of them are money, cash, currency, and dough.''

• ''By the way, a coin has two sides, a right and left. It all depends on how you look at it.''

• ''There is hardly anything you can have without money, except happiness, love, and everything nature gives.''

• ''In our country, some people make their own money, but they go to jail.''

Successful writers *can* make money from their efforts, although most books are not commercial successes. To help our books earn us more money we not only have to write better, we need more ''POBs.''

322. *Husband* (turning off the TV and picking up a book): You know, dear, I'm really a POB.

Wife: A POB? What's that?

Husband: Well, you know what an SOB is—a son of a bitch.

Wife: Sure, but what's a POB?

Husband: A Print-Oriented Bitch. POB.

Wife: I get it. But why are you that?

Husband: We're both POBs. We love books. Look at the advantage of a book. It can't come unplugged. There's nothing to blow out or get out of order. It's always available, even in bed. You can stop and think about it, or even argue with it, anytime you want. And it is never interrupted by commercials.

On to another aspect of writing. Probably nothing turns readers off faster than clichés, old worn-out expressions. Read the next ''story'' and you'll never write another cliché.

323. A girl at the Lincoln School in Providence, R.I. wrote the following verses to illustrate what clichés are:

B.C. (Before Cliché)	A.D. (After Discovering 'em)
Morning	*Morning*
I watched a fluffy cloud drift by Across the boundless blue sky And saw the sun's rays, molten gold, Upon the dewy earth unfold.	I saw the sun with battered face Trying to warm the human race; I watched a sodden cloud limp by Like some discouraged custard pie.
Evening	*Evening*
I felt my fettered soul uplift Before the rosy sunset drift, And in the hazy blue afar I saw the gleaming evening star.	The sleepy sun in flannels red Went yawning to its western bed; I saw one shivering small star No brighter than our dishpans are.

Writers have to deal with editors. Me, I'm a great lover of editors. They are one of the non-secrets of my success. Here's a story about an excellent piece of editorial judgment.

324. It's an old story among newspaper writers, but it's worth repeating. A young reporter happened to be in Johnstown, Pa., during the terrible flood of 1889. He started his dispatch thus: "God sat on a hill here last night and watched disaster and death sweep through this community."

His editor promptly wired back: FORGET THE FLOOD—INTERVIEW GOD.

But editors can be damned by authors, although usually it's the authors who are wrong.

325. The famous editor George Horace Lorimer (1868–1937) rejected a manuscript sent to him by a hopeful author. The angry author wrote back to Lorimer: "You rejected my story without even reading it. How do I know you didn't read it? Because as a test I pasted together pages 16, 17, and 18, and when the manuscript came back the pages were still pasted together. What a way to edit—to reject things you haven't even read!"

Lorimer replied, "Dear _____: At breakfast when I open an egg, I don't have to eat the whole egg to discover it is bad."

And then, of course, there are literary agents. I've seldom used one, but many authors do, sometimes with great resentment *after* they become recognized and popular.

326. A once-famous author, anonymous now, left this provision in his will: "I direct that 10 percent of my ashes be scattered over my literary agent."

327. Fred Allen (1890–1954), author of many works including *Only Yesterday* and *The Lords of Creation*, wrote: "You could take all the integrity in Hollywood, put it in the navel of a flea, and still have room left over for an agent's heart and a caraway seed."

Even though I know that *A Treasury of Humor* is not Bartlett's *Familiar Quotations*, I cannot resist, while on the subject of writers, setting down some of my favorite *un*familiar writing. John Bartlett (1820–1905), please excuse me!

328. Some of the most humorous comments about human behavior and human nature come in short blips, not in full-blown stories. For years, as I have listened and read, I've jotted down items that appealed to me. Here are a few of the best:

Authors Known

- W. N. P. Barbellion (1889–1919), British biologist: "I take pride in my Simian ancestry. I like to think that I was once a magnificent hairy fellow living in the trees, and that my frame has come down through geological time via sea jelly and worms and Amphoxius, fish, dinosaurs and apes. Who would exchange these for the pallid couple in the Garden of Eden?"

- Ashley Montagu (1905–   ), British-born American anthropologist, writing in 1981: "Science has proof without certainty. Creationists have certainty without proof."

- Dr. Samuel Johnson (1704–84), the author of the *Dictionary of the English Language* (1755), was frank in personal relations and exact about the distinctions between words, but not very particular about cleanliness. When a woman at supper remarked with disgust, "Dr. Johnson, you smell," he replied, "Nonsense, good woman. It's you who smell. I stink."

- Paul Lacey, Dean of Faculty at Earlham College, Richmond, Indiana, in 1982: "Chairing a meeting of the Earlham faculty is like trying to take eighty kangeroos for a walk."

- Flora Lewis, columnist for *The New York Times*, criticizing simplistic, cure-all "solutions" to complex political, economic, national, and world problems: "I am a rock-ribbed, hard-nosed, knee-jerk, bleeding-heart moderate."

- Richard Cardinal Cushing of Boston: "Saints are all right in heaven, but they're hell on earth."
- Mark Twain (1885–1910) on a modern painting: "It looks like a tortoise-shell cat having a fit in a platter of tomatoes."
- E. B. White (1899–1985): "To plant asparagus, dig a ditch three years ago." (*Note*: A useful point for long-term planners.)

Authors Unknown

- "To copy from one book is plagiarism; to copy from three is research."
- "Before you give a colleague a piece of your mind, be sure you can spare it."
- An elderly Quaker at the end of a truly *silent* Meeting for Worship, commenting to a friend: "I am glad that those who had nothing to say refrained from giving verbal evidence of the fact."
- "My dear, we live in a time of transition," said Adam to Eve as they left the Garden of Eden.
- "Some are born great; some achieve greatness; and some just grate upon you."
- "I always start a book in the middle. I get more out of it that way. I not only wonder how it's going to end; I also wonder how it began."
- A child's definition of heredity: "Uh, well, it's like, you know, if your grandfather didn't have any children, and your father didn't have any, probably you wouldn't have any children either."
- From a British schoolboy's essay on Johann Sebastian Bach (1685–1750): "Johann Sebastian Bach was a most prolific composer. He was the father of twenty children. In his spare time he practiced in the attic on a spinster."

• "The only function of economic forecasting is to make astrology look respectable."

I close this chapter with a masterpiece—an unintended masterpiece. A former student of mine, who taught school in New England, was so delighted when he received this essay that he called me up and dictated it to me over the phone. "Note the honesty," he said. "And the ingenuity; and the sentence variety; and the plain, frank, sophisticated humor." He concluded: "It's what I'd call giving it a good try even though you don't know anything about the subject!" I advise you to read it slowly and savor each word and all the subtle verbal rhythms.

329.   *The Owl*
                    [by a fifth-grade girl]

The bird I am going to write about is an owl. I don't know much about the owl so I am going to write about the bat. The cow is a mammal. It has six sides, right, left, an upper and a lower. At the back it has a tail on which hangs the brush. With this it sends the flies away so they don't get in the milk.

The head is for the purpose of growing horns and so that the mouth can be somewhere. The horns are to butt with and the mouth is to eat with. Under the cow hangs the milk. The milk comes and there is never an end to the supply. How the cow does it I have not yet realized but it can make more and more.

The cow has a fine sense of smell and you can smell it far away. This is the reason for the fresh air in the country. The man cow is called an ox. It is not a mammal.

The cow does not eat much but what it eats it eats

twice so that it gets enough. When it's hungry it moos and when it says nothing it's because its inside is full up.

The End

10.

Organizations: Government, Business, Legal . . . and Others

It's sometimes hard to laugh at (or with) organizations, because people who get habituated to their own organization often develop peculiar jargons, procedures, and pomposities. In most organizations, much of the humor is in-house. But, to start, here are a few out-of-house bits.

330. A plumber wrote to the Bureau of Standards, saying that he found hydrochloric acid excellent for cleaning drains. He inquired whether the Bureau thought it was okay. Their answer: "The efficiency of hydrochloric acid is indisputable, but the chlorine residue is incompatible with metallic permanence."

The plumber wrote back thanking the Bureau and expressing his pleasure that they agreed with him.

The people at the Bureau were alarmed that they had been misunderstood, so they replied: "We cannot assume responsibility for the production of toxic and noxious residues with hydrochloric acid, and we suggest you use an alternative procedure."

The plumber wrote again, saying that he was glad they were keeping in touch, and was happy to know about their responsibilities, and that he was continuing to use HCL.

The Bureau sent a final communication, a telegram: "DON'T USE HCL STOP IT EATS HELL OUT OF THE PIPES."

Franklin D. Roosevelt would have enjoyed the Bureau of Standards' telegram; to wit:

331. During World War II, President Franklin D. Roosevelt (1882–1945) objected to the blackout posters printed by the authorities in Civil Defense: "Illumination must be extinguished when premises are vacated." FDR's reaction: "Damn, why can't they say 'Put out the lights when you leave?' "

Sometimes citizens who want to cooperate or even get jobs with the government misinterpret routine questions.

332. An applicant for a job with the federal government was filling out the application form. He came to this question: "Do you favor the overthrow of the United States government by force, subversion, or violence?" Thinking it was a multiple-choice question, he checked "violence."

And it's not just the federal government.

333. An Affirmative Action official of the State of Pennsylvania wrote to a business officer of a company whose policies were being investigated: "Please send to this office a list of all your employees broken down by sex."

Some time later, this reply was received: "As far as

we can tell, none of our employees is broken down by sex.''

But back to the federal government.

334. Sometimes, if you are like me, you wonder whether government jargon is at all comprehensible, especially the jargon of its health-care organizations. It's very hard, for example, to figure out what medical expenses you did or did not get reimbursed for. So it is nice to see that administrators occasionally get their basic concepts straight. According to the *Atlanta Journal and Constitution*, the Director of Health Care Financing Administration wrote: ''Death is the ultimate negative patient health outcome.''

Perhaps one might use the acronym for this expression and say of a friend who died, ''She experienced UNPHO.'' Could it be addictive?

Even large commercial establishments, which, unlike governments, depend on customers to make a profit, have language trouble.

335. We all sometimes get lost in large department stores or buildings and need careful directions. Sometimes these directions are especially intriguing, as in the case of the man who wanted to find the men's shoes area. He asked at an information desk, and the clerk there told him, ''Go up that escalator; get off at the next floor; turn left and make your way through ladies' intimate apparel, and turn right.''

It's government organizations, usually local ones, that have the grim responsibility of carrying out capital punishment. This used to cause more language problems than it does now, but there were ways to get around them by sounding "organizational."

336. In the olden days, it was sometimes hard to explain to others the electrocution or hanging of a relative without bringing disgrace to the family. Here, however, are two suggestions that proved satisfactory:

electrocution: He occupied the chair of applied electricity at one of the larger state institutions, and died in harness.

hanging: He died at a public ceremony when the platform on which he was standing gave way.

Banks, which are *very* organized, are not immune to language goofs.

337. The chairman of a bank reported to the officers and staff members that the institution was "on the brink." The next year, however, he said he was glad to inform them that the bank "has taken a step forward."

Even in distant Australia routine organizational questions cause embarrassment.

338. Australia was first colonized by convicts from Great Britain. This started in 1788, but by 1850 free colonization had replaced the old penal settlements. Recently, a tourist was entering Australia, where one of the routine questions border guards ask is, "Do you have a criminal record?"

"Oh, I'm dreadfully sorry," replied the tourist, who

had read a little history, "I had no idea it was necessary."

Let's now turn to a weighty question: How does one succeed in organizations?

339. A wise observer once counseled a younger employee who was angry over a colleague's thoughtless behavior: "Never ascribe to malice what can be perfectly well explained by stupidity."

And a real toughie: How can a person succeed as the head of a modern university?

340. Henry Merritt Wriston, president of Brown University from 1937 to 1955, described what university presidents' jobs are like:

"The president is expected to be an educator; to have been at some time a scholar, to have judgment about finance, to know something of construction, maintenance and labor policy, to speak virtuously and continuously in words that charm and never offend, to take bold positions with which no one will disagree, to consult everyone and follow all proffered advice, and to do everything through committees, but with great speed and without error."

I suppose one could make the same comment about the heads of other institutions. But it's not the heads who most frequently make trouble. There's a certain middle-level type.

341. There are at least two sorts of people who work in complex organizations like governments, businesses, and schools: those who, when a problem reaches them, contribute to its solution; and those who, when a problem comes to them, escalate it into something worse. A man of the latter type was called into the chief executive's office and told, "John, don't be an embolus."

"A what?" asked John.

"A blood clot—something that circulates through the system causing trouble."

Yet another sort of organization is football. Perhaps it will help us attain a better perspective on our addiction to this violent game by seeing it from an outsider's viewpoint.

342. Many years ago, a Chinese scholar had been invited for a term at the University of Pennsylvania. His academic host, thinking that the Chinese ought to have a good understanding of the customs of American students, invited him to a football game. The Chinese scholar watched the game with great interest and some signs of puzzlement. At half-time he turned to his host and asked, "Why don't they hire coolies to do it?"

Some wag once said, "All organizations were set up to extinguish the principles for which they were founded." This is, I know from experience in schools, service organizations, and even publishing houses, not always true—although one is often tempted to think that it is.

343. A zoning board had just been set up in a new community. A householder went to the office to re-

quest permission to build a small toolshed in his back-
yard.

"Have you a plan?" asked the director.

"Oh, yes," said the householder, who showed him
a map of his neighborhood, the dimension of his yard,
and a sketch of the shed.

"That looks fine," said the director. He pulled out
a piece of paper, wrote a few words on it, Xeroxed it,
and said, "Here's your permission."

A month later, a neighbor in almost exactly the
same situation also wanted permission for a shed in
her yard. She went to the director, got as far as a
secretary, and made her request. "Thank you, Mrs.
Smith," said the secretary, taking the documents.
"Telephone me in two weeks and I'll let you know
what the director's decision is, or what further steps
are necessary."

"But," groaned Mrs. Smith, "a month ago my
neighbor got permission right away."

"Oh, yes," said the secretary, "but that was before
we got organized."

It can indeed be slow working things through organizations. Doubtless, that is part of living in a democracy
where everyone's opinion should count. However. . . .

344. Arleagh D. Richardson III was director of the
National Humanities Foundation in Concord, Massachusetts. His work, which he did diligently and well,
involved reporting to and seeking consensus in a great
many committees. When he died, one of his admirers
suggested this epitaph for him: "He has gone to another meeting."

Perhaps we should be glad that there are meetings, and lengthy discussions, and that everything is not run with 100 percent efficiency.

345. According to a story of uncertain origin, an efficiency expert was hired to make a report on the New York Philharmonic Orchestra. As a part of this preparation, he attended several concerts. At last, he issued his report, which read in part as follows:

Report on the New York Philharmonic Orchestra

''For considerable periods, the four oboe players have nothing to do. Their number should be reduced and the work spread more evenly over the whole of the concert, thus eliminating peaks of activity. . . . All twelve first violins were playing identical notes. This seems unnecessary duplication. . . . Much effort was absorbed in the playing of semiquavers. This seems an excessive refinement. It is recommended that all notes be rounded up to the nearest quaver. . . . No useful purpose is served by the repeating on the horns a passage which has already been played by the strings. . . . It is estimated that if all redundant passages were eliminated, the whole concert time of two hours could be reduced to twenty minutes and there would be no need for an intermission.''

I find it useful to tell the above story to parents and school trustees. Too often they tend to think that students' minds are simply empty vessels to be filled with information in the most efficient manner possible. But, thank God, our minds are much more than passive containers. They *think*, reject, distort, improve, and ennoble, just as a symphony, even a cacophonous one, ennobles the notes of a scale.

One more bit about efficiency, although here no expert was involved.

346. Possibly you remember the antics of George Burns (1896–) and Gracie Allen (1923–1964), the comedy team who played the endlessly patient husband and the scatterbrained wife. A true story about Gracie Allen—at least it's said to be true—recounts that a repairman, called in to fix her electric clock, said, "There's nothing wrong with the clock. You didn't have it plugged in." Gracie replied, "I don't want to waste electricity, so I only plug it in when I want to know what time it is."

But enough of efficiency. Let's get onto something tougher. A day's work in a hard-pressed organization can be tough. Was the father in the following story telling the truth?

347. Father sparrow came home from work looking terribly battered, feathers every which way. Mother sparrow asked, "Wow! You look terrible! Where have you been?"

Father sparrow: "It was terrible. On the way home from work I got mixed up in a badminton game."

It's obvious that organizations need personnel—that means *people*. And one of the functions of personnel is to deal with paperwork. But paperwork can become so routine, mysterious, or esoteric that a bureaucrat loses his sense of perspective and function.

348. A junior officer at the Pentagon was a hard worker, and he had a very nice well-furnished office.

However, he began behaving strangely. First he shoved his desk out into the space also occupied by his secretary's desk. Then a few days later, as he was leaving for the day, he pushed his desk out into one of the many long corridors. He worked there for a few days, and then he shoved his desk into the men's room and set up work there.

All of this had not escaped the notice of his fellow workers. It seemed more and more strange to them, so strange that they did not dare ask the officer himself what he was doing. Instead, they went to the division psychiatrist and asked him to ask the officer.

So the psychiatrist walked into the men's room, sat on the edge of the officer's desk and asked, "Why have you kept moving your desk? Especially, why into the men's room?"

"Well," said the officer, "I figure that this is the only place in the Pentagon where they know what they're doing."

Another office story:

349. In a large office full of administrators sat a worker at his desk, his *in* and *out* boxes practically overflowing. Yet he did not look the least bit harried. On the front of his desk was a sign that read: THE BUCK PAUSES HERE AND, HAVING PAUSED, MOVES ON.

Paper shufflers sometimes acquire an inflated sense of their own importance.

350. A flea was riding on an elephant's ear. After a while, they crossed a wooden bridge, which wobbled badly and almost collapsed. When they got safely to the other side the flea said to the elephant, "Boy, didn't we shake that bridge!"

One *does* need a sense of proper perspective in organizations, whether they be religious or medical.

351. A priest took a group from his parish out hiking, and they got caught in a furious thunder-and-lightning storm. As they crouched under some shelter, with the storm getting worse and worse, a parishioner said, "Father, can't you do something?" The priest replied, "Sorry, I'm in sales, not management."

And a similar event: A patient in a nursing home was put on a bedpan. The nurse said, "When you want to get off, please report to the management."

Sometimes the highest management officer needs to provide the lowliest functions and services.

352. A headmaster once told a conference that a school head is like a fire hydrant. The audience looked puzzled, so the speaker explained, "You know, good for putting out fires—and whatever."

Here's another that shows how low organizational procedure and attitudes can fall.

353. The head of a well-known school was suddenly struck with a severe illness and rushed to the hospital. The next evening a regular monthly meeting of the school trustees was held. Someone proposed that an official minute be passed expressing hope for the head's speedy recovery. It passed nine to eight.

So school heads can be unpopular, at least with their boards. The same with big businessmen—sometimes with surprising results.

354. A very unpopular but powerful businessman died. Two of his "friends" saw the obituary notice and decided to go to his funeral. When they arrived, they found the church very crowded.

"My God!" said one. "Look at all these people. How do you explain it?"

"Well," said the other, "give people what they want and they all show up."

The variety of organizations that constitute the law and the courts also generate some negative feelings among ordinary people.

355. A witness to an automobile accident was testifying. The lawyer asked him, "Did you actually see the accident?"

The witness: "Yes, sir."

The lawyer: "How far away were you when the accident happened?"

The witness: "Thirty-one feet, six and one quarter inches."

The lawyer (thinking he'd trap the witness): "Well, sir, will you tell the jury how you knew it was exactly that distance?"

The witness: "Because when the accident happened I took out a tape and measured it. I knew some stupid lawyer would ask me that question."

As yet, I don't know how Heaven is organized—perhaps I never will. But one must assume that if heaven exists, someone must be in charge, and one would expect a beautiful sense of perspective and proportion from that Someone. But, can we be sure?

356. A fairly common complaint made about doctors, and to a lesser degree about nurses, is that they are often in too much of a hurry. Perhaps this is inevitable, given the demands made upon them. Doctors tend to have the additional annoying habit of regarding themselves as infallible. Since two of my children are doctors, I can't go along with this, but against me is the experience of a man who arrived at the gate to Heaven. As he was negotiating with Saint Peter, he noticed a small fellow riding madly around on a bicycle, carrying a black bag.

"Who's that on the bicycle?" the man asked Saint Peter.

"Oh," replied Saint Peter, "that's God. He thinks he's a doctor."

Yes, doctors are important, and they are to be revered for the remarkable discoveries they've made.

357. This story takes place some time in the future, when transplant surgery has become so successful that even brain transplants are possible. An ambitious young businessman seemed to be losing his energy and ideas and went to his doctor for a checkup. After consulting with specialists, the doctor reported, "Rupert, I'm afraid you need a new brain—a transplant."

"My God," exclaimed Rupert. "I've heard about those. But, uh, how much do they cost?"

"Well," the doctor replied, "it depends on what kind of brain we implant. A lawyer's brain is about $15,000. A good medical brain is $30,000. Then there's an army officer's brain. That costs $60,000."

"But that's preposterous," said the patient. "How can an army officer's brain cost twice as much as a doctor's brain?"

"An army officer's brain is as good as new," said the doctor. "it's never been used."

(Note: You may change around the professions to suit your own experience or biases)

We'll close this chapter with a story that demonstrates the simplemindedness of the United States immigration service. I'm sure there is truth in this story because the family of my many-year, thousands-of-miles jogging companion had a similar experience. Their name was Rachkovitch, but it was written down by immigration officials, despite protests, as "Rock." So I jog with Eli Rock.

358. In the early twenties, three Jews emigrated to the United States. As so often happened in those days, the American immigration officials at Ellis Island simplified their complicated names on the official records. In this case, the three were recorded as Diamond, Gold, and Taylor. Many years later, they met and asked how each of them had done.

Diamond: Oh, I've done very well. With my name I started a jewelry store. Right from the start it was successful. Now there are Diamond Jewelers all over the country.

Gold: Well, brother Diamond, I, too, have succeeded. Same idea. Gold? So I started the Gold Ornaments Shop. The shop succeeded wonderfully. The branches spread. Now I'm a millionaire.

Taylor: With me it wasn't so simple. My name is Taylor, so I started a clothing store. I worked very hard, but it failed. So I started another, but it also failed. My family, they were starving. So what could I do but pray to God. "Oh, Lord," I said, "Help me to prosper. Lord, if you do, I'll promise to give you 50 percent of the profits."

Diamond and Gold: Well, tell us. Did it work?

Taylor: Did it work? You never heard of Lord and Taylor?

So, long live enterprise! It's what makes organizations work.

11.

Fund-Raising

Raising money for worthy institutions like schools, universities, and community organizations is hard and noble work—it therefore has its humorous aspects. Some of the stories that follow may even be useful in upping the take, directly or indirectly. One of the most important things for a fund-raiser to remember is that people give money because they *want* to, not because they are forced to. The following story demonstrates the wrong approach.

359. A new patron was dining in a very expensive restaurant. As she was having a before-dinner drink, she saw a waiter hurry by with a serving of flaming shish kebob.

"What in Heaven's name is that?" she asked her companion.

"Oh," he replied, "that's just a customer who left only a twenty-dollar tip."

What we need is the happy generosity of the man described below:

360. A very fat woman got on a crowded bus. She stood in the aisle, looked around, and loudly complained, "Isn't anybody going to give me a seat?"

A thin man stood up and said, "I'll be glad to make a contribution."

Let's return to some stories that illustrate the wrong approach to raising money. You can ask for *too* much.

361. A young man took his girlfriend out to a restaurant. After the meal he was studying the bill at some length, and his girl observed him with concern. "Gary," she asked, "you look sick. Is it something I ate?"

Another mistake is to *pretend* that we know the donor very well and use first names inappropriately.

362. Heintz Loeffler, now a well-known businessman, was a Rear Admiral during World War II, and he is so listed in various directories. One day he received a letter from a respected charity that began, "Dear Rear . . ."

The next two stories illustrate what happens when one puts on too much pressure.

363. In some communities it is the custom to give a Christmas present of a few dollars to the trash collectors. It's gone so far that some collectors tape an open envelope to trash cans: "Season's Greetings from Your Trash Collectors."

One family somehow neglected to respond to the "greetings." Just a day or two before Christmas, there appeared another envelope: "Season's Greetings from

Your Trash Collectors.'' And under that, writ large: ''Second Notice.''

364. Three-year-old Molly was playing in the living room, testing things out, and her mother saw her pick up a nickel, examine it, and then swallow it. The mother rushed to her, turned her upside down and pounded her on the back. Molly caughed up two dimes. The mother was frantic, and she shouted to her husband outside, ''Molly just swallowed a nickel and coughed up two dimes. What shall we do?''

The father yelled back, ''We can use the money. Keep feeding her nickels.''

Sometimes sharing dreams makes people feel they want to give.

365. A woman was having a dream: A tall, sinister man was approaching her bed. In terror, she asked him, ''What are you going to do?''

The man smiled slightly, ''That's up to you, lady. It's your dream.''

Let's not forget that we have to be sure that the person from whom we're asking money actually has some money to give.

366. A burglar entered a house in the middle of the night. He was interrupted when the owner awoke. Drawing his gun, the burglar said, ''Don't move or I'll shoot. I'm hunting for your money.''

''Let me turn on the light,'' replied the victim, ''and I'll hunt with you.''

367. The following really happened to me: I was helping with a telethon for Germantown Friends School and I was making an appeal to a former student of mine, now a doctor. He said he'd give the same generous amount he'd given last year. When I asked whether he could possibly up it by 25 percent or so, he replied, "I can't. I have a parasitic infection."

"Oh, Joe," I said. "I didn't know that. I'm terribly sorry. What have you got?"

He laughed, "A new daughter."

I have found, though, that doctors, once they get beyond the parasitic-infection stage of life, are sometimes very good at giving—as well as asking for—money. As in medicine, especially surgery, expertise is important.

368. Two surgeons, Dr. Rhoads and Dr. Weisberg, were highly competent, prestigious medical men, devoted not only to their professions but also to the important task of raising money for their university. They were discussing a couple of excellent prospects for major gifts, and Dr. Rhoads was explaining various methods of giving: annuity trusts, unitrusts, gifts of tangible property, insurance policies with benefit to the university, and so forth.

"Wait a minute," said Dr. Weisberg. "I know all about scalpels and forceps and clamps and retractors and scissors, but I find it very hard to keep these money-raising arrangements straight in my mind. Is there any general term one can use to describe them?"

"I suppose," said Dr. Rhoads, "you could just call them *instruments of extraction*."

One of the most effective means of "extracting" money is to suggest a "multi-year pledge." But it doesn't always work.

369. An 81-year-old woman, an alumna of a fine school, was asked by a younger alumna to make a contribution to their school's fund-raising campaign. The older woman said she'd be glad to make a gift.

"That's wonderful! Would you like to make that into a pledge over three years?"

"A pledge?" said the elderly woman. "Why, at my age I don't even buy green bananas anymore."

Of course, not everybody is devoted to giving to charity. One can hope that the girl in the following story will become better—or more nobly—educated.

370. One Sunday, a girl was given two quarters as she left for church, one for the collection plate and one for herself to spend as she wished. As she walked to Sunday school she was playing with the quarters in her hand, and one dropped on the street and rolled through the grates of a sewer. The girl looked down into the watery depths and said sadly, "There goes God's quarter."

For a major fund-raising to succeed, people have to give more than just income. But, I'm sad to say, there is a strong conviction in parts of American society that capital is sacred.

371. A writer was visiting a small New England town to get background material for a novel. As he walked around talking with people, he noticed that there was one man whom everyone avoided as they passed him. The writer finally asked one of the citizens who the fellow was.

"Please don't ask," replied the citizen. "We just don't talk about him in the town."

Even more puzzled, the writer went into the local newspaper office and asked the editor, "Who is this man—a murderer, a rapist, a thief, what?"

The editor grew tense and said in a low voice, "No, none of those. The town could live with that. He [whispering] dipped into his capital."

Here's a story about a delightfully naive child. To apply it to fund-raising, for *bones* read "researching the prospect" and for *skin* read "money."

372. A small girl was told she needed an X-ray. When she came out of the X-ray room, she told her mother, "They took a picture of my bones."

"Yes, dear," replied the mother. "Did everything go all right?"

"Sure," said the girl. "It was amazing. I didn't even have to take my skin off!"

Despite all the cautions suggested by many of the stories in this chapter, there's no doubt that devotion, persistence, and even strength are needed for effective fund-raising.

373. The strongman at a circus sideshow demonstrated his power before a large audience. Toward the end, he squeezed the juice from a lemon between his hands. He then said to the audience, "I will offer $200 to anyone in the audience who can squeeze another drop from this lemon.''

A slight, scholarly-looking man came forward, picked up the lemon, strained hard, and managed to get a drop. The strongman, amazed, paid the man and asked, ''What is the secret of your strength?''

''Practice. I was treasurer of the Methodist Church for thirty-two years.''

12.

Problems of Life

If life gave us no problems, we probably wouldn't need humor, and that would be a tragedy. Don't look for a nicely articulated scheme of organization in this chapter, or you'll have yet another problem. After all, life doesn't send us its problems organized. But life *does* send problems, even to cows.

374. Two contented cows were grazing in a field when they looked up and saw a shiny, handsome milk truck drive out of the dairy lane. On the truck was painted:

FRESH MILK
pasteurized
homogenized
irradiated
vitamin D added

One cow said, "Did you see that truck?"
"Yeah," mooed the other.
"Makes you feel pretty inadequate, doesn't it?"

Feeling inadequate is no fun. Perhaps it's healthy from time to time just to complain, at the start or at the end of the day.

375. A man came into the office one morning looking very depressed. His colleagues asked him what the trouble was. "I'm suffering from a sexually transmitted disease."

There was embarrassed silence until somebody dared ask what it was.

"It's called life."

376. A man came home from work, sank down into a chair, and groaned to his wife, "I wish I was dead—or a reasonably accurate facsimile thereof."

Sometimes children, quite unconsciously, can give us wonderful advice. The following happened to a friend of mine.

377. Stephen Cary was painting his long picket fence, watched by a small neighbor, Carol. Steve had been painting for hours, it seemed, and he still wasn't even half finished. He sighed, "Carol, I'm so discouraged. I've been painting so long and look how far I have to go."

"I don't see why you're so discouraged," Carol replied. "You only have to paint one picket at a time."

But there *are* situations where even the one-at-a-time philosophy won't work.

378. One woman had so many problems that her life was like that of a thousand-legger wearing loose socks.

You see, every time the thousand-legger pulled two socks up, 998 fell down.

Socks, at least for human beings, don't give us as many problems as other inanimate objects do. You doubtless have heard of Murphy's Law (Whatever can go wrong *will* go wrong). But have you heard of the *IPIO Principle*?

379. A number of years ago, a friend of mine, an engineer, invented what he called the "IPIO Principle." IPIO stands for the Innate Perversity of Inanimate Objects. The IPIO principle explains why spoons fall bowl-up into the dishrack, thus holding their water, why, when you're putting a pan away in the lower cupboard, the upper one bangs you in the head; why on a trail in the woods, roots have a mind of their own and reach up to trip you when you're looking at a bird; or why a slimy pile of dog poop puts itself on the sidewalk in the only place you can pass between a wheelchair and two businessmen in animated blinding conversation.

And another story about the IPIO Principle, this one with a bit of animation injected.

380. Sometimes life, even the most enjoyable parts of it, seems to get out of control through absolutely no fault of our own. At such times, it's helpful to think of Alice in Lewis Carroll's (1832–1898) *Through the Looking-Glass* (1871). You remember she was playing croquet, using a flamingo as a mallet and a rolled-up hedgehog for a ball. The bird kept turning its head to look at her with a "who, me?" expression, and the hedgehog ball had ideas of its own.

The IPIO Principle came up while I was working on this book. Before I started, I had a lifetime's collection of humorous stories. By the time I had finished what you hold here, the stories were logically arranged and an index was made. As I did a final reading before sending the book off to the publisher, I found, to my horror and dismay, that somehow two story numbers had IPIOed their way into the text without any stories attached to them. Oof! To readjust the whole book to include these numbers would mean hours, nay days, of work, and dull work, too. So you will see just below how I dealt with the problem. It may even be the best part of the book, because it will enlist my readers' help in getting ready to write the sequel to *A Treasury of Humor*. . . .

381. HELP!!
1. IPIO Principle at work.
2. Now, even if your name is Murphy, think up a humorous story.
3. See number 382 for where to send it.

382. Send humorous stories to:

Eric W. Johnson
IPIO Victim
6110 Ardleigh Street
Philadelphia, PA 19138
Thanks!

Now, ask yourself if the IPIO principle is at work in the next story.

383. A worker was leaning far out over the edge of a high building in the middle of a crowded city. *Unfortunately*, he slipped and fell. *Fortunately*, there was a haywagon proceeding slowly down the avenue just below him. *Unfortunately*, there was a pitchfork sticking, prongs up, in the middle of the load of hay. *Fortunately*, the man didn't hit the pitchfork. *Unfortunately*, he didn't hit the haywagon either.

And here's a similar story, the hero of which certainly knew how to take a positive view of events.

384. An old man fell out of the window of a twenty-story building. As he passed the fourteenth floor a friend yelled, "Hey, Mike, how's it going?" Mike shouted, "Okay, so far!"

Many years after the final outcome of the two preceding stories, another problem could have arisen, assuming that the men involved had some loving friends and family that survived them.

385. My wife and I were driving through California listening to the radio. A commercial message came on from a place called The Woodlawn Cemetery. A man with what my wife calls a "plummy voice" raised a question that had never occurred to me before to worry about. He asked, "Is seepage disturbing your loved ones?"

Certainly, as we have seen, one of the problems of life is fear of death. It can be a strong motivator, especially when nature helps.

386. One of the popular activities in Florida is jungle-cruise boat rides. People love the low overhanging vegetation, the thick growth in the water, and the snakes and alligators. One experienced cruise guide was asked, "Do you ever have trouble with snakes dropping into the boat from overhanging branches?"

"Nope," said the guide, "there's no problem. You get a snake in the boat, and then you get people in the water. You got people in the water, so you got alligators, so you get people back in the boat. So, you see, nature at work, no problem."

And if it's not fear of death that motivates you, it may be simply the fear of pain. Can sharing that fear help prevent pain?

387. A woman who had had some painful experiences in the dentist's chair went one day for a check-up and was told she would need a major filling. As the dentist laid out his materials and prepared to drill, the woman reached under the dentist's white coat and gently took hold of his testicles.

"Madame," said the dentist, "what *are* you doing?"

"Well, doctor," said the woman, "we wouldn't want to hurt each other, would we?"

Here's one that involves an even more serious threat to a doctor, this time by a younger patient.

388. The pediatrician was preparing to take a blood sample from six-year-old Tommy, who looked very scared. As the doctor came closer with the needle, Tommy started to cry. So the doctor, hoping to distract the boy, smiled and asked, "Well, Tom, what are you going to do when you grow up?"—and he stuck the needle in.

Tommy replied, "I'm going to kill you!"

Let's move quickly now to another problem, anti-Semitism, certainly not a life-and-death matter these days in the USA. But it does exist, and here are two examples of dealing with it.

389. During World War II, a society lady who lived on Philadelphia's exclusive Main Line decided to be charitable and support the war effort by inviting three soldiers to Thanksgiving dinner. She called the nearby army base and was connected with a sergeant. He heard the lady's invitation and said he'd be glad to send three soldiers. Then the lady added, "Sergeant, I don't want any of them to be Jews."

"I understand, Madame," said the sergeant.

So on Thanksgiving, there stood on the doorstep of the fine Main Line house three immaculately uniformed soldiers, all of them black. "We're here for Thanksgiving, Madame," said one, politely.

The lady was astonished. "But, but . . . ," she sputtered, "the sergeant must have made a mistake."

"Oh, no, Madame," said the soldier, "Sergeant Cohen never makes a mistake."

390. Groucho Marx (1895–1977) was Jewish, but he married a gentile. Once he phoned an exclusive swimming club in Beverly Hills to find out why his son Arthur had just been barred from membership. "My son is only half Jewish," said Groucho, "so he could go in up to his bellybutton, no?"

The next story is a below-the-bellybutton story that couldn't have happened anywhere but in France. When my wife and I stayed there for two years in the early 1950s, we were occasionally able to take a few days off from work to tour the country. A couple of times we stayed in magnificent castles, with luxurious rooms, but the facilities became totally primitive when we made our way down long corridors to *la toilette*, or *le W.C.* It was the same just after World War I.

391. An American soldier had become very fond of France. After the Great War's armistice was signed, he decided to spend a few weeks there before returning home. He traveled into the Vosges Mountains, southeast of Paris, a region of low rounded mountains and beautiful views. With delight, he came to a small pension situated on the very top of a hill. The Madame in charge showed him to a comfortable room, explained when meals were served, and left him to enjoy. After a time, he needed to go to the bathroom, but he couldn't find one. He went downstairs and knocked on a door marked, "Privé." The Madame answered "Oui, Monsieur? Qu'est-ce-que vous voulez?" The soldier, somewhat embarrassed, struggled to get out the words, "Où est le W.C.?"

The woman took him out on the porch, swept her hand toward the view, and said, "Voilà, Monsieur, toute la France." ("There, sir, all of France.")

Here's another problem of life, from another country. How many of your problems are like this?

392. An Australian bushman was given a new boomerang. The trouble was, he spent the rest of his life trying to throw the old one away.

And speaking of trying to get rid of things, consider this from our by-now old friend Mark Twain.

393. Mark Twain (1835–1910) tells the story of trying to get rid of a wreck of an old umbrella. First he threw it in the ash can, but someone recognized it as his and returned it. Then he dropped it down a deep well, but someone repairing the well saw the umbrella and returned it. He tried several other methods, but always the umbrella came back. "Finally," says Mark Twain, "I lent it to a friend, and I never saw it again."

This story recalls a comment by Henry Wadsworth Longfellow (1807–1882): "I find that my friends are very poor arithmeticians but excellent bookkeepers."

The next four stories deal with quite practical methods for dealing with certain problems: borrowing (again!), unmarked country roads, desert islands, and catching fish with worms.

394. Mrs. Grannum accused her neighbor Mrs. Johnson thus: "Mrs. Grannum, when you returned my eggbeater, I found you had broken it. What are you going to do about it?"

Mrs. Johnson replied: "That's ridiculous. In the first place, I never borrowed your eggbeater. Furthermore, it was in good condition when I brought it back. And, anyway, it was broken when you lent it to me."

395. A tourist stopped his car on a country road and asked a young boy, "How far is it to Smithville?"

"Well," said the boy, "the way you are going, it's about 24,996 miles, but if you turn around, it's about four."

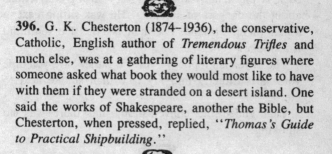

396. G. K. Chesterton (1874–1936), the conservative, Catholic, English author of *Tremendous Trifles* and much else, was at a gathering of literary figures where someone asked what book they would most like to have with them if they were stranded on a desert island. One said the works of Shakespeare, another the Bible, but Chesterton, when pressed, replied, "*Thomas's Guide to Practical Shipbuilding.*"

397. Two experienced fishermen went ice-fishing. They chopped holes in the ice about twenty-five feet apart, put worms on their hooks, dropped their lines in the water, and got nary a nibble. This went on for several hours, but no luck. Midafternoon, a schoolboy arrived, walked confidently onto the ice, and chopped his hole between those of the two men, and caught fish after fish.

The men were amazed, and finally one approached the boy and asked, "Tell me, young man, what's your secret?"

The boy replied, "Mmmm yymmm mmms wmmm."

"What's that?" asked the man. "Say it again, please."

The boy: "Mmmm yymmm mmms *wmmm.*"

The man: "I'm sorry. I just can't understand you. Would you speak a little more clearly?"

At that, the boy cupped his palms, spat a large amount of substance into them, and said clearly, "Keep your worms warm."

Sometimes people try to solve problems by using very forceful language, in both speaking and writing.

398. A physician I know has very strong convictions about the dangers of smoking. He was sitting next to a man on an airplane. The man asked, ''Do you mind if I smoke?''

The physician replied, ''Sir, I'd rather have you pipe your farts directly into my face than smoke next to me.''

That ended the conversation, and there was no smoking.

399. A seed company that was offering prizes to people who sold their products received the following letter:

''Dear Sir:

''You are a chisler and a cheat. You were suppose to send a baseball glove like the one in the picture. You dident. You were suppose to send an extra prize also. You dident.

''Your enemy,
''Roy—

''P.S. Remember when I get mad I stay mad.''

Roy, it must be admitted, took a somewhat naive, simplistic approach to trying to solve his problem. The next three stories show a similar, though less violent, naiveté. The first can be used to demonstrate urgency.

400. A young girl awoke early and, as she was going downstairs to get something to eat, the grandfather clock struck seven. But it didn't stop there. It went right on striking: 8, 9, 10, 11, 12—and still it didn't stop: 13, 14, 15 and so on. The girl ran back upstairs shouting to the whole family, "Get up! It's later than it ever was!"

The next demonstrates a deeply-felt psychological, emotional need.

401. Nine-year-old Jane said to her father in a moment of sharing, "Dad, I'd like to feel, you know, that I'm *really needed*."

"I understand, Janey," replied her father, "but keep in mind that people who are really needed are asked to do a lot of different things."

"Yeah, I guess I see," said Jane. "What I want is to feel *needed* but not have to *do* anything."

And the third shows a desire to protect people from harm, or to sympathize with their plight.

402. A small girl, while waiting for her meal, wandered quietly around the restaurant. She stopped at a table where a couple had been served two platters of raw oysters. The girl stared, horrified, and then asked, "Are you going to eat those, or have you?"

She reminded me of the old saying, "He was a brave man who first ate an oyster."

A good many people deal with their problems, and those of others, with "fresh" comments.

403. A judge who had sentenced a criminal to twenty years in prison said, in dismissing him, "Peace be with you, my man."

The man replied, "Peace on you, too, Judge."

404. Some members of a health club were having their first meeting. The director of the group said. "Now, I'd like each of you to give the facts of your daily routine."

Several people spoke, admitting their excesses, and then one obviously overweight member said, "I eat moderately, I drink moderately, and I exercise frequently."

"Hmm?" said the manager. "And are you sure you have nothing else to add?"

"Well, yes," said the member, "I lie extensively."

405. Dorothy Parker (1893–1967) was the mistress of witty insults. At one party she got stuck in a very long, dull conversation with a woman who wouldn't stop her stream of gossip. At last, Parker pointed far across the room to a man she saw stifling a tremendous yawn, and said, "We'd better stop, dear; I think we're being overheard."

At another social occasion someone held a door open for Parker and said loudly, "Age before beauty." Dorothy swept through the doorway remarking equally loudly, "Pearls before swine."

And while we are considering Dorothy Parker:

406. Dorothy Parker was the author of light verse, including such volumes as *Enough Rope* and *Death and Taxes*. She wrote:

"Drink and dance and laugh and lie,
    Love the reeling midnight through,
For tomorrow we shall die!
    (But, alas, we never do!)"

Parker lived to be 74. Not bad!

Perhaps it's a long way from Dorothy Parker to the mountains of Switzerland, but you'll see that the problems of life can reach high altitudes.

407. Swiss mountain guides who always do the same trails can get tired answering the same questions over and over. One time an English tourist was giving his guide an especially hard time with silly questions. They were walking through a mountain valley that was strewn with rocks, and the traveler asked, "How did these rocks get here?"

"Sir," said the guide, "they were brought down by a glacier."

The tourist peered up the mountain and said, "But I don't see any glacier."

"Oh, really?" said the guide. "I guess it has gone back for more rocks."

Sometimes problems of frustration can be eased by gentle—or not-so-gentle—insults.

408. I've long been comforted in my baldness by the old cliché that "grass doesn't grow on a busy street." I tried this one on a man about my age who had a splendid head of hair, but he wryly replied, "I always say, 'There's no sense in putting a roof on an empty shed.' "

409. *A classic modern-day riddle:* If you see something dead lying in the road, how can you tell whether it was a lawyer or a rattlesnake?

Answer: That's easy. If there are skid marks before the dead body, it's a rattlesnake.

(Feel free to substitute for lawyer any other professional you wish to insult!)

We don't generally like rattlesnakes—or skunks—even though both creatures have what it takes to survive in a hostile environment. Recently, I learned about an extension of skunkery, a substance called skunk oil. Some mischief-makers or criminals squirt it onto the seats and floors of movie theaters when they want to take revenge against the proprietors. But not everybody knows what it is. The employee in the next story tried to cover up his ignorance by asking questions.

410. A man went into a department store and asked a salesman, "Do you have any skunk oil?"

"Skunk oil?" said the salesman.

"Yes, skunk oil," said the man.

"For men or for women?" asked the salesman.

There are other people, some very young, who make no effort to cover up their ignorance—or their omniscience.

411. A three-year-old girl used to reply to any statement made to her with, "I know." For example, "The world is round." ("I know.") "People should always tell the truth." ("I know.")

One day the girl's older brother said to her, "You always answer, 'I know.' "

"What's wrong with that?" asked the girl.

"Well," said her brother, "only God knows everything!"

The girl replied, "I know."

It's fun, if one doesn't overdo it, to look at humorous stories that have a regional aspect. Take the way some Vermonters deal with life's problems.

412. Vermonters may not be what they used to be, and perhaps they never were, but their thrift habits are wittily described in a collection by Walter Hard, *A Matter of Fifty Houses*. Here are three items:

- One Vermonter kept a bag in his attic—it was labeled, "Pieces of string too short to use."
- A man named Eber was counting his change with great care. Finally, a fellow citizen asked him, "Given enough?" And Eber replied, "Jes' barely."
- A Vermonter had promised some summer people to finish work on their house by the end of August. When they arrived, they were very displeased, for they had heard many solemn promises. In annoyance, they asked, "Why is the work not done as you promised?"

   The reply: "Well, I'll tell you. August didn't turn out to be as long as I calculated."

413. A tourist driving through Vermont greatly admired the magnificent bulls he saw. At one point he saw an especially wonderful animal, stopped his car, took out his camera, and climbed a fence to get a prize photo. Just then he saw a farmer looking at him. "Hey, there," said the tourist. "Can you tell me? Is that bull safe?"

The farmer's reply was direct. "A darn-sight safer than you are, mister."

And there's another region Down East.

414. A man in Maine who for many years made part of his living as a trapper was talking to a visitor about "conservation people" who called trapping "inhumane." "I have a theory about those folks," he said. "When someone hasn't anything much worth doing, they decide to take up reforming. First they find something that won't interfere with their style of living, and then, brother, *can they reform!*"

415. During World War II, when U.S. soldiers were very obvious and numerous in England, an American asked an English lady, "Why is it you don't like us Americans?"

The lady replied, "You're over-loud, you're overpaid, you're oversexed, and you're over here."

And another *région* is France. They have their problems, too, and not all of them have to do with the W.C.s.

416. The French enjoy eating rabbits as a delicacy. Occasionally, though, a low-grade restaurant (of which there are very few in France) will substitute cat meat or rat meat for rabbit. Once my wife and I were in a small French restaurant looking at the menu, and we were struck by one of the entreé listings. It was rabbit, with an elaborate and delicious-sounding sauce. At the end of the description was written: "Guaranteed rabbit. We serve the head." ("Lapin guaranti. On sert la tête.")

Another sort of region, not nearly so far removed from normal life as some of us like to think: mental hospitals and insane asylums. The man in this story had very definite ideas about the region between his hands. Was he joking?

417. A visitor was permitted to walk freely through an insane asylum and became interested in observing a man who was moving about slowly. The man's hands were held together as if he were hiding something in them.

"Pardon me, sir," said the visitor, "but I'm interested. What are you hiding in your hands?"

"Try to guess," said the insane man.

"A million dollars?"

The man peeked into his hands. "Nope," he said.

"An airplane?"

Another peek. "Nope!"

"A yacht?"

Another peek. "Nope!"

"A horse?"

Another peek, and then a sly look at the visitor. "What color?"

Enough of life's problems? I guess so. Therefore, let's stop with a story about mediocrity, one about self-righteousness, and then a pleasant hope for avoiding *all* problems!

418. One of the original ideas in our Declaration of Independence: It guarantees citizens of the United States "life, liberty, and the pursuit of happiness." Benjamin Franklin (1706–1790), who helped draft the great document, pointed out later that all our nation guarantees is the *pursuit* of happiness. "You have to catch up with it yourself," he said.

Another wise man, Kenneth Boulding, professor of economics at the University of Colorado, has something more to say about the pursuit: "If you pursue excellence, happiness sneaks up behind you and touches you on the shoulder. If you pursue mediocrity, you're sure to catch it."

419. An annoyingly self-righteous man went to the doctor for a check-up. He said, "I feel terrible. Please examine me and tell me what's wrong with me."

"Let's begin with a few questions," said the doctor. "Do you drink much?"

"Alcohol?" said the man. "I'm a teetotaler. Never touch a drop."

"How about smoking?" asked the doctor.

"Never," replied the man. "Tobacco is bad and I have strong principles against it."

"Well, uh," asked the doctor, "do you have much sex life?"

"Oh, no," said the man. "Sex is sin. I'm in bed by 10:30 every night—always have been."

The doctor paused, looked at the man hard, and asked, "Well, do you have pains in your head?"

"Yes," said the man. "I have terrible pains in my head."

"O.K.," said the doctor. "That's your trouble. Your halo is on too tight."

420. One of the wittiest, most pleasant good wishes I have ever heard was uttered by a fellow named Kemmons Wilson. "As you slide down the banister of life," he said, "may all the splinters be pointed in the right direction."

13.

Old Age

All of the stories in this chapter came to me by way of old people themselves. I gathered them while doing research for my book *Older and Wiser: Wit, Wisdom and Spirited Advice from the Older Generation* (Walker Publishing Company, New York, 1986). The elderly, I found, can see a greater number of humorous dimensions to life than any other age group. So: "Grow old and humorous along with me, the good-better-best is yet to be!" say I, to misquote Robert Browning's (1812–1889) *Rabbi Ben Ezra*.

Old people are too often considered to be a pretty sad and miserable lot. But according to a 1981 Harris poll, this perception is simply false. The poll showed that most oldsters don't suffer as much as most people—including other oldsters—think they do. Consider these figures:

Problems a Person Might Have	Percentage of the General Public that Thinks Elders Suffer from the Problem	Percentage of Elders Who Say They Actually Do Suffer from the Problem
loneliness	65%	13%
not feeling needed	54%	7%
poor health	47%	21%
not enough jobs	51%	6%
not enough medical care	45%	9%

not enough to do	37%	6%
poor housing	43%	5%
not enough friends	28%	5%
Average percentage	45%	5%

But enough! This is a book of humorous stories about the human condition, and I've been getting a bit nonhumorous. Besides, you may be thinking, "Figures don't lie, but liars can figure," or, as Benjamin Disraeli (1804–1881, Prime Minister of Great Britain, 1868 and 1874–1880) put it, "There are three kinds of lies: lies, damned lies, and statistics."

Here's one statistic—plus a related comment.

421. When I asked an 85-year-old man what made him feel most hopeless about life at his age, he wrote: "Danged if I can think of what in my life makes me feel hopeless. Life is a bowl of cherries, and if you have to pick out a few ants along the way, that's the way it is."

This reminds me of what Benjamin Franklin (1706–1790) wrote at age eighty-four: "People who live long, and who will drink the cup of life to the very bottom, must expect to meet some dregs."

Let's face it, no matter how good old age is, no one (yet) has lived forever. So it's surprising that old people don't spend a lot of their time thinking about the subject: Only 24 percent of oldsters say they fear death (whereas 75 percent of those polled in junior high school list death as one of their top five worries or fears).

Here's a practical attitude toward death.

422. In England, an old man was asked by a friend, "Now that you've retired, what do you do?"

"I have a good routine," said the old gent. "My man brings me a cup of tea and *The Times*. I drink the tea, read the obituary column, and if I'm not in the obituaries, I get up."

Here's another approach, this time from an American woman whose greatest interest was in living.

423. A son was talking with his very old mother about what inevitably lay ahead, her death. He stumbled a bit and then said, "Mother, you're getting along in age, and who knows what may happen? I mean, shouldn't we make a few decisions about arrangements?"

There was a silence, the mother smiling calmly. So the son went on, "I mean, Mom, do you want to be buried or cremated?"

The mother replied, "Well, son, I don't know. Why don't you just surprise me?"

It's enjoyable to know how some famous people felt about the prospect of death. Let's consider John Quincy Adams, Voltaire, and H. G. Wells.

424. The great American lawyer, orator, and politician, Daniel Webster (1782–1852) was visiting John Quincy Adams (1767–1848), sixth President of the United States, when Adams was about 80. Webster asked Adams how he was feeling. The old man replied, "I inhabit a weak, frail, decayed tenement, battered by the winds, and broken in upon by the storms. From all I can learn, the landlord does not intend to repair."

425. The French philosopher and writer Voltaire (1694–1778) was a leading figure of the Enlightenment, a hater of injustice, and a lover of pleasure. His masterpiece *Candide* (1759) ends with this line: "Let us cultivate our garden."

When Voltaire was on his deathbed in Paris, he seemed to those around him to be comatose. Then a draft from the window made a gas lamp flare up brightly, and Voltaire said, "Aha! Already the flames!"

426. When H. G. Wells (1866–1946) was on his deathbed, his friends and relatives were around him trying to get some "last words." The great writer whispered with great impatience, "Can't you see I'm busy dying?"

Perhaps that should be enough about death. Here are two stories about where to live when you're older. Both contain a certain amount of cheerful wisdom about retirement communities.

427. Two elderly ladies, Matilda and Rosie, were chatting over tea one day. Matilda had recently moved to a retirement home. Rosie asked, "Matilda, how do you like your new home?"

"Oh, I love it," answered Matilda. "There's so much to do, and no burdens of cooking and cleaning."

"I'm not sure I'd like it," Rosie said. "I understand there are hardly any men at those places."

"Oh, indeed there are," said Matilda. "There's Will Power, and Charlie Horse, and [whispering] you can even go to bed with Arthur Itis. *And*, if you don't like them, there's Ben Gay."

428. Two ninety-year-old men in a retirement community were deeply involved in a chess match, when one of them looked up and noticed a small woman running naked down the hallway. "Look at that!" he exclaimed. "I must say Sally certainly needs to have her dress pressed."

Sometimes we wonder about the mental capacity of elders. There's no doubt—at least in *my* mind—that elders grow wiser with age. But one must admit that short-term memory declines, like the memory of names or of what we did five minutes ago, or even of what we are supposed to do now.

429. Old age has its problems, and many elders meet them with frankness and strength. A 77-year-old woman told me about three women who were having tea together. One of them said, "You know, the funniest things are happening to me. I sometimes find myself at the bottom of the stairs and wonder whether I was going up to get something or was coming down to get something."

The second woman replied, "You know, I sometimes find myself in front of the refrigerator. I can't remember whether I just put something in or I have come to take something out."

The third woman said, "Well, I don't have anything like that happening to me yet. But perhaps I'd better knock on wood"—which she did, three times. Then, startled, she looked at her guests and said, "I guess somebody's at the door. Excuse me!"

430. An eighty-year-old woman was told by her minister that, at her age, she should be giving some thought to what he called "the hereafter." She said to him, "I think about it many times a day."

"Oh, really?" said the minister. "That's very wise."

"It's not a matter of wisdom," she replied. "It's when I open a drawer or a closet, I ask myself, 'What am I here after?'"

But old people can also be pretty sharp, and even brief, as these two stories show.

431. Winston Churchill (1874–1965) retired from government life in 1955, but, as was his privilege, he would come back to the House of Commons from time to time to observe. One day, when he was well into his eighties, he dropped into the House and was being helped down the aisle to his seat by two aides. They were whispering behind his back: "The old fellow's getting pretty feeble." "I hear he's becoming a bit soft in the head." "Yes, I hear he's completely dotty."

As Churchill eased into his seat, he turned to the men who were helping him and snarled quietly, "Yes, and they say also that he's getting hard of hearing."

432. Throughout his life, Somerset Maugham (1874–1965) was bothered by a hesitation in his speech. He was invited to address one of the most prestigious groups in England on his eightieth birthday. After dinner he rose, thanked his hosts, took a sip from his glass of water, and began, "Old age has many benefits . . ."

There followed a long and painful pause, while he turned to the head table for help, sipped some more water, shuffled his notes, and several times started to speak. At last, holding the audience firmly in his grasp, he said, "I'm trying to think of some," and sat down.

We don't think of old people as fashion designers. Somehow, one has the impression that designers must die young. Here's at least one exception, a sharp one at that.

433. At age 86, Gabrielle "Coco" Chanel (1883–1970), the French fashion designer, said to a reporter: "I will tell you that my age varies according to the day and the people I happen to be with. When I'm bored, I feel very old, and since I'm extremely bored with you, I'm going to be one thousand years old if you don't get the hell out of here at once."

One of the problems oldsters must be cautious about, especially since they are so much wiser, is overdosing others with advice.

434. An anonymous seventeenth-century nun wrote down this prayer: "Lord, thou knowest better than I know myself that I am growing older and will some day be old. Keep me from the fatal habit of thinking that I must say something on every subject and on every occasion. Release me from craving to straighten out everybody's affairs. Make me thoughtful but not moody, helpful but not bossy. With my vast store of wisdom, it seems a pity not to use it all, but Thou knowest, Lord, that I want a few friends at the end."

Another way to lose friends and not influence people is to talk first and think afterwards.

435. An 81-year-old woman, asked what "old" means, said, "I guess old people think more, feel more, and empathize more. *But* I still get impatient and sometimes put my tongue in gear before I engage my brain."

What about old age and brotherly love, a noble type of love? Here's a realistic view of it.

436. The preacher was delivering a sermon on brotherly love. He was suddenly struck with the idea of asking the congregation this question: "Can any of you honestly say that you don't have a single enemy? If so, will you please stand up?"

There was a pause and thoughtful silence. Then an old man stood and said, "Here am I. I have no enemies."

The preacher and congregation were pleased, and there followed a tribute to the old man, at the end of which the preacher asked him, "And what is your secret?"

The man replied with a fierce grin, "I outlived all the SOBs."

And then there are other sorts of love besides "brotherly." What kind of love is shown in the next story?

437. An older couple regularly attended church. The pastor was much impressed by how harmonious and how in love they seemed. They always held hands all through the service. One day after church, the pastor couldn't resist going up to them to express his admiration. He said, "I find it so inspirational to see how deeply in love you are, even, after all these years, holding hands like that."

The wife looked up sharply and said, "It's not love, Pastor, I'm just keeping him from cracking his knuckles."

Then there is marital love, the finest, noblest kind, according to me. The next three stories demonstrate aspects of it—high, factual, and low.

438. To celebrate their fiftieth wedding anniversary, a couple returned to their honeymoon hotel. After retiring to bed, the wife said, "Darling, do you remember how you stroked my hair?" And so he stroked her hair. She reminded him of the way they had cuddled, and so they did. Then, with a sigh, she whispered, "Won't you nibble my ear again?"

With that, the husband got out of bed and left the room. "Where are you going?" cried the wife.

"To get my teeth," he said.

439. There was a young woman who was very much interested in marrying this wealthy old gentleman. After he proposed, she suggested, "We might even have some children!"

The old gentleman replied, "Oh, no, my parents won't let me."

"What do you mean?" asked the young woman. "Who are your parents?"

He replied, "Mother Nature and Father Time."

440. A related story: An old woman who was talking with a friend about her 102-year-old father, saying that she couldn't keep an appointment because she had to go to his wedding. "My goodness," said her friend, "I'm amazed that at his age he'd want to get married."

The old woman replied, "Who said he *wanted* to get married?"

So much for love. What about health? One of the big medical controversies today is whether old people benefit from drinking alcohol. The next story, I'll admit, does not teach a clear lesson about this.

441. A rather prominent man, who had served his community well, reached his ninety-fifth birthday, and newspapers sent out reporters to interview him. One asked, "To what do you attribute your long, wonderful life?"

The old man replied, "I have never taken a sip of alcohol nor smoked a single cigarette."

At that point, a noise of joyful singing and banging was heard from upstairs.

"My God!" said a reporter. "What's that?"

"Oh," said the 95-year-old, "that's my dad enjoying one of his periodic drunks."

High blood pressure and cholesterol-clogged vessels are a problem of old age.

442. An eighty-year-old friend of mine was sent to the hospital for an operation to improve his poor circulation. When asked by a friend just exactly what had happened in the hospital, he explained, "They stuck this thing up my artery into my heart and took out twenty years worth of rice pudding."

Perhaps one of the ways to keep your health is to maintain an optimistic—or at least realistic—attitude toward your troubles.

443. According to studies I have made, elders enjoy much better health than most people think they do. For example, Bruce Bliven, at age seventy-nine, wrote: "I have calculated that the diseases I don't have outnumber those I have by twenty to one, so I am only 5 percent ill."

However, a 77-year-old man wrote to me: "I seem to be in good health, though getting out of bed in the mornings makes the raising of Lazarus look like a cheap trick." (As you probably know, Lazarus was the brother of Mary and Martha. According to *John*, Chapter II, Jesus raised Lazarus from the dead.)

Another man said, "You know you're getting older when in the morning you hear snap, crackle, pop, and it isn't your breakfast cereal."

And the great pianist and composer Eubie Blake (1883–1983) said at age 93, "If I'd known I was going to live to be this old, I'd've taken better care of myself."

To your health! But not in excess.

14.

Drama: Conductors, Actors, and Directors

The stage and screen have always been wonderful sources of humor. Here are some odd bits of humor that came out behind the scenes. First some music stories:

444. Everything was going well during the orchestra rehearsal until a trombonist played a wildly cacaphonous *toot*! The conductor angrily objected, and the trombonist said humbly, "I'm sorry, sir, I played a fly."

And now, from the ridiculous to the sublime.

445. One of the greatest conductors of all time was Arturo Toscanini (1867–1957), whose skill was shown during a rehearsal of Claude Debussy's (1862–1918) *La Mer*. He wanted to achieve an especially spiritual effect in one passage. His vocabulary in English was not vast, and he was at a loss for words to describe exactly what he wanted the orchestra to do. So he took a large white silk handkerchief from his breast pocket and threw it high into the air. Every player in the group was hypnotized as the handkerchief floated softly, sensuously to the floor.

'There!'' Toscanini said, smiling. ''Play it like that!''

The next story concerns a matter that is as *un*delicate as the floating handkerchief was delicate. But it still relates to the dramatics of music, and it also involves Toscanini.

446. Madame Schumann-Heink (1861–1936) was a terrific, broad-bodied contralto. At one performance of the New York Philharmonic Orchestra, conducted by Arturo Toscanini, Schuman-Heink entered from the rear of the stage and proceeded down the center aisle between the players. But she was so large that she was banging into all the music stands.

Toscanini, seeing what was happening, whispered loudly to her, ''Sideways! Go sideways!''

''Mein Gott!'' replied Schumann-Heink. ''I got no sideways!''

447. Lauritz Melchior (1890–1973) was perhaps the leading Wagnerian tenor of his day. In Wagner's opera *Lohengrin* (1850), the hero rescues and marries Princess Elsa but is doomed to leave her. During the climax of one performance at the Metropolitan Opera House, Melchior, dressed in white armor, was downstage singing his last farewell to Elsa, after which he was supposed to board the swan boat and be carried tragically, majestically away. There was a brief pause between phrases of the song, and just as Melchior was about to go into the climax, some stagehand mistakenly pulled the lever that sent the swan boat off, leav-

ing Melchior on stage. At this moment, people in the
wings heard Melchior whisper loudly backstage, ''Pardon me, but what time does the next swan leave?''

We move now to an experience I had during college
with a very well-known conductor of the Harvard Glee
Club, Archibald Davidson. (A freshmen classmate of
mine, Leonard Bernstein, was the general-purpose accompanist for the Glee Club, and even then we were
impressed with his ability to play anything with total facility, and even modesty.)

448. In 1937 the Harvard Glee Club was rehearsing
Bach's *St. Matthew's Passion*, directed by Archibald
Davidson. The group was singing a beautiful, complex
passage when Davidson held up his hands. There was
immediate silence and the conductor said, ''Hark! I
heard a voice!'' We looked puzzled and Davidson explained. ''What I want, and what makes this Glee Club
great, is homogenous mediocrity.''

I might add that when *St. Matthew* rehearsals were
scheduled with the Radcliffe Choral Society, the *Harvard Crimson* announcement read tersely, ''Tonight,
7:30, Sanders Theater, joint Passion with Radcliffe.''

Obviously, one of the main elements in drama is actors. They often act humorous parts and illuminate our
understanding of the human condition, but sometimes
they are humorous *outside* of the roles they are acting.
Here are three examples:

449. Jackie Coogan (1914–1984) was a young star in
the film version of Charles Dickens' *Oliver Twist*. In
one scene Coogan was supposed to start crying real

tears when one of the boys in the orphanage asked him, "Where's your mother?"

His reply was a sobbing, "My mother is dead," but Jackie just couldn't make the tears come. The director, Frank Lloyd (1889–1960), said to him, "Just try to imagine that your mother is really dead."

But, try as he would, Coogan still couldn't make the tears come. Finally, he asked, "Mr. Lloyd, would it be all right if I imagine that my dog is dead?"

450. An actor was testifying in a criminal case. To the lawyer who was cross-examining him he said, "I am the greatest living actor of all time."

"What?" said the lawyer. "How can you make such a statement?"

"Well," said the actor, "I am under oath. I don't want to commit perjury."

451. Lynn Fontanne (1889–1983) and Alfred Lunt (1893–1977), two famous actors, were married in 1922 and starred in many sophisticated comedies together in the theater, television, and the movies. One time Fontanne went to see a preview of one of their films and came home to Alfred in great distress. "Alfred," she cried, "in our new film we look terrible. You have thin lips; and I have grayish hair, sunken cheeks, bad teeth, terrible posture, and look like an old hag!"

Lunt listened, and then there was a long pause. He looked at Fontanne and said, thoughtfully, "Thin lips, eh?"

452. Argentine businessman Juan Potomachi, who died in 1955, wrote in his will that he had always wanted to be on the stage but never had the opportunity, due to his position in the community—and his lack of talent. He left $50,000 to a scholarship fund for young actors, with one proviso:

"My only condition is that my head be preserved and used as a skull in Hamlet. My dearest wish would be thereby fulfilled after all, as I would still have a part in a play after my death."

Another kind of drama takes place in courtrooms. This story tells of a judge who did not recognize the emotional force of drama.

453. In a criminal trial the defending lawyer gave a most moving, elequent, impassioned appeal for his client. He didn't cite any relevant evidence, but he emphasized what a disaster it would be for the defendant, his wife, and small children if he were found guilty. One could almost say that there was not a dry eye in the courtroom. The judge, realizing that no evidence had been presented, said in stern tone, "I hereby instruct the jury to ignore what has just been said."

One juror leaned toward another and remarked, "You can't unring a bell."

We shall bring this chapter to a close with two stories about film directors, who are quite unlike musical conductors, I think. Directors are certainly terribly important, and their task often is a tough one. Sometimes, though, they talk too much and want to direct everything—and now and then they get their comeuppance.

454. Cecil B. DeMille (1881–1959), the famous Hollywood director of *King of Kings* (1927), *The Crusades* (1935), and *The Greatest Show on Earth* (1952), often talked too much, especially to the movie extras involved in his films. Each day before lunch break, he'd lecture them: "Now I want everybody's complete attention," and then he would speak at length from a platform, through a mike.

During one of these lectures he noticed two women in the assemblage talking. "Stop!" DeMille said, pointing. "Ladies, you two come up here, please."

The two women mounted the platform.

"If what you have to say is so important, please tell *everybody* over the microphone."

One of the women shyly took the mike and said, "I was just asking my friend who was that old, baldheaded, son-of-a-bitch, and when's he gonna let us have lunch?"

DeMille was shocked. He grabbed the mike and yelled, "Lunch!"

Before we declare "Lunch!" for this chapter, let's have one more story about directors, one that leads beautifully into the next chapter, "History," which, according to a well-known account started, "In the beginning. . . ."

455. One of the great American film directors was John Huston (1906–1987), whose films included *The Maltese Falcon* (1941), *Moby Dick* (1956), and *Annie* (1982). But perhaps the toughest assignment he ever had was the modestly titled film *The Bible* (1966). He found the Creation and Ark sections especially challenging. When a friend asked him how things were going, he replied, "I don't know how God managed. I'm having a terrible time."

15.

History

Whether "history is bunk" (Henry Ford [1863–1947]) or "a fable agreed upon" (Napoleon Bonaparte [1769–1821]), it is certainly full of humor, as these few side-swipes show.

Humor is not the same as laughter, although it often results in laughter. And, except for hyenas, human beings are the principal species that laughs. Here is some perspective on laughter. History, especially evolution, is all about perspective, after all.

456. In his classic but too-explanatory book *Enjoyment of Laughter* (1936), Max Eastman (1883–1969) writes of people, dogs, and evolution: "Man has been defined as the laughing animal, but that is not strictly accurate. Dogs laugh, but they laugh with their tails. And a tail is an awkward thing to laugh with, as you can see by the way they bend themselves half double in extreme hilarity trying to get that rear-end exuberance forward into the main scene of action. What puts man on a higher stage of evolution is that he has got his laugh on the right end."

So laugh alone or with others, as you consider these long- and-short-term views of history, the first of which concerns a very famous American event.

457. When an "Indian"—as Christopher Columbus (1451–1506) called the natives of the lands he "discovered"—saw Columbus walk ashore, he remarked to his Native American friends, "Well, there goes the neighborhood."

And the neighborhood *went*. Here's one about a Native American who tried to reverse the process.

458. In 1986 Edward Guilmette, an Iroquois Indian from the Mohawk tribe, told a class of fifth graders at the Learning Project school in Boston that a member of his tribe had recently visited Spain. The children were well aware that Columbus had landed in a world already inhabited by thousands of people with a rich culture, even though he stuck a flag in the sand and said, "I claim this land for Spain."

"Well," said Guilmette, "my brother tribesman put a Mohawk flag on a beach in Spain and said, 'I claim this land for the Mohawks.' "

"What happened?" asked the eager children.

Guilmette replied, "It didn't work."

Archeologists are historians of a sort, and they work hard to determine the significance of the relics and remains of past human life. It's important that they discriminate carefully.

459. In the years after the tomb of Egyptian King Tutankhamen (c.1350 B.C.) was found almost intact

(1922), Egyptology became a "hot" field, and excavations became even more common. One of the most knowledgeable people about the excavations was the late John A. Wilson, a professor of Egyptology at the University of Chicago. He related this story: An archeologist in Egypt was asked by a sly American tourist to identify a gnarled dessicated object the American had eagerly fetched from a cave in the Valley of the Kings. The archeologist carefully examined the object, and replied, "Some creep crept into the crypt, crapped, and crept out."

Here's another way to interpret archeological remains.

460. At the Philadelphia Academy of Natural Science there is a vivid exhibition of Egyptian mummies. One of the mummies is especially impressive, most of it well-wrapped. But the remains of the face and eye sockets show, the teeth are visible, and the ribs and bits of skin remain. Our young daughter was fascinated by the sight of this 5000-year-old body, and after a few minutes turned to us and remarked, "Dad and Mom, that man is sick!"

Perhaps, accustomed as we are to considering history as a record of major events, we may forget that small things can be very important, too. First, let's look at such things in the life of one individual.

461. The young daughter of William Howard Taft III was assigned to write a short autobiography, as was each child at the start of a new grade. Here's what she wrote: "My great-grandfather was President of the United States [27th president, 1909–1913]. My grandfather (Robert Alphonso Taft, [1889–1953]) was Senator from Ohio. My father is Ambassador to Ireland. I am a Brownie.''

And here are some items of history from an even more circumscribed point of view:

462. Fifth graders at a small Friends' school in Frankford, Pa., were working on a project that was supposed to give them a sense of history. Each one was asked to do a personal ''time line'' from ages 0 to 10 or 11. The following selection could give us older people a sense of what is *really* important in history. (The parentheses indicate the age at which each event occurred; the spelling is as written—not bad for fifth graders.)

(1) My mom stuck my face in my cereal because I kept spitting at her.

(1) My daddy stuck a pin in me.

(1) Smeered choclate icing in my hair.

(1) Stuck head in cake.

(2) I was potty trained.

(2) First scary movie.

(2) spilled laundry detergent all over the basement.

(3) I fell asleep with a book on my head.

(3) Sister gave me a shiner.

(3) Ate the eyes of the cookiemonster.

(3) I went pee in my pants and my sister was born.

(4) I fell down sement steps.

(4) first Tricicul

(4) Met my best friend Jenny. I cried every day. (That was stupid.)

(6) I lost my first tooth.

(6) I didnent cry when school started.

(6) My grate gradmom died.

(7) quit tap acro

(8) Mom and Dad divorced.

(9) I was a jack in the box for halloween.

(9) Won McDonald's french fries.

(10) flew to Calafonya.

But now we go back from today's fifth-grade history to the "prehistoric" Stone Age, beginning about two million years ago and continuing for a long time, even to the days of cavepeople.

463. We have all heard of the cavemen, but not so much of the cavewomen. Be that as it may, the magnificent cave paintings of the Paleolithic period, the Stone Age (c. 14,000–9,500 B.C.), are vastly impressive. Since, as myth will have it, the cavemen were out all day hunting for food—and probably picking their teeth—it was the cavewomen who stayed at home, cared for the kids, and painted the walls in whatever spare time they had. One day one of these artists turned to her companions as they painted and said, "Isn't it strange that none of the great painters of the world have ever been men?"

People moved out of caves (as a matter of fact, a very small portion of humankind ever lived in caves—there weren't enough to go around) and learned to get about. They even crossed the English Channel.

464. In the course of his many duties and pleasures, King Henry VIII (1491–1547) had reason to cross the English Channel, a notoriously rough passage. Once he had just landed in England after a very choppy crossing. Green-faced and dizzy, he said to one of his courtiers, ''Yesterday, all was fair, a glorious Sunday, but this sick transit spoils the glory o' Monday,'' a clever pun on the Latin *stc transit gloria mundi*, ''so passes away the glory of the world.''

Somewhat later, people even moved across the continent of North America, sometimes with litigious results.

465. When railroads were first built across the plains, cattle, which were unused to them, were often hit by locomotives. When the cattle were described in claims against the railroads, they were always described as ''full-blooded, very valuable stock.''

The claims department of the Union Pacific Railway brought this up with their chief. He, being a philosopher, said, ''Well, I don't see what can be done about this. I've come to the conclusion that nothing improves the quality of livestock as much as crossing it with a locomotive.''

Locomotives have long since been replaced by airplanes as the primary method of traveling across this country.

466. Today, we usually feel quite secure as we fly, but back in the 30s it may not have been so safe. Here are a set of instructions from one of the first manuals for stewardesses—now called ''flight attendants'':

(1) Keep the clock and altimeter wound up.

(2) Carry a railroad timetable in case the plane is grounded.

(3) Warn the passengers against throwing their cigars and cigarettes out the windows.

(4) Keep an eye on passengers when they go to the lavatory to be sure they don't mistakenly go out the emergency exit.

Most people, perhaps we Americans as much as any, tend to see history and world events from a self- or nation-centered viewpoint—as is suggested by the following stories.

467. One day Ralph Waldo Emerson (1803–1882), one of America's greatest thinkers and philosophers, was visited by a local farmer, who saw a book by Plato (427?–347 B.C.) in Emerson's library and asked to borrow it. When the farmer returned the book, Emerson asked him how he liked it. The farmer replied, ''I liked it. This Plato has a lot of my ideas.''

468. There are a good many institutions of higher learning that believe themselves to be the timeless center of the world. One of these is Oxford University in England. One afternoon in the Senior Common Room, the members of one of the colleges were discussing how to invest some college funds. The college's financial officer said, ''I recommend land. It has proved to be a very good investment over the last thousand years.''

There was a general murmur of approval and nodding of heads, except for one history don [professor], who commented, ''Yes, that may be, but you must remember that the last thousand years have been quite exceptional.''

469. At Khartoum, capital of Sudan, on the banks of the Nile, is Gordon College, named for the famous British General Charles Gordon (1833–1885), who was killed there in 1885, resisting a siege. In the college garden stands a magnificent statue of Gordon mounted on a camel. Gordon is pictured in full military dress, and the camel is wearing rugs and tassels.

A British civil servant who was stationed at Khartoum for many years used to take his son from time to time to see and admire the general. They would always stand together in silence for a moment looking at the imposing statue. Finally, the time came when the civil servant was to be transferred. Before they left, he took his son for a final visit to Gordon. As they turned away, the father's eyes moist with tears, his son looked up at him and asked, "Tell me, Father, I've always wondered, who is that funny-looking man on Gordon?"

But now we come to an account of a fresh historical perspective born out of desperation.

470. The famous humorist Robert Benchley (1889–1945), author of many works, including *My Ten Years in a Quandry*, showed his sense of humor early. He was a student at Harvard and had taken a course in international relations. Benchley, whose mind was agile but who didn't do much serious studying, came into the exam unprepared and was faced with this question: "Discuss the influence of the northern fisheries case upon international relations."

Benchley pondered a bit and then began his essay: "I shall discuss the northern fisheries case from the point of view of the fish."

But leave it to that wise, holy, revolutionary, nonviolent man Mohandas K. Gandhi to give us Westerners a sense of perspective.

471. A reporter asked Mahatma Gandhi (1869–1948), "What do you think of Western civilization?"

Gandhi replied, "I think it would be a good idea."

Another wise man, Benjamin Franklin, we have heard from before in this book. He had sound ideas about what influences history—and what might improve the future.

472. When the town of Franklin, Massachusetts, decided to name itself after Benjamin Franklin (1706–1790), its leaders sent the wise old man in Philadelphia this rather bold letter: "We have named our town after you, and we should like a donation of a sum of money from you in order that we may put a bell in the town hall steeple."

Benjamin Franklin's reply was both insightful and kind: "I am very much honored, very glad indeed to send you a sum of money, only don't buy a bell with it. Buy a public library because I have always preferred sense to sound."

So, what does promote truth? Certainly sense more than sound. But then, perhaps not. Consider this account:

473. Some fourth graders were studying a unit on Greek mythology, especially Apollo and his great sources of truth, the oracles. The most revered oracle was the one at Delphi, whose sayings had unquestioned authority. In a test on the unit, one of the questions was to define the Delphic Oracle. A child wrote, "The Delphic Oracle was a woman who sat on a hole in the ground and gave forth wisdom."

If we no longer have oracles, except self-proclaimed ones who probably contain more vanity than truth, where can we go to find Truth? One modern man made a major, strenuous search, with a surprising result.

474. A Westerner went to the mysterious East to find out the meaning of life and Earth's true place in the universe. The man climbed up a high mountain, where an Eastern sage sat in a cave, meditating. After a respectful wait, the Westerner asked, "Oh, Sage, can you tell me? What is Earth's true place in the universe?"

The Sage replied, "The Earth stands on the back of the Great Earth Turtle."

"Aha!" said the Westerner. "And what does the Great Earth Turtle stand on?"

The Great Earth Turtle stands on the back of the Great Universal Turtle."

"Hmmm!" mused the Westerner. "And, oh, Sage, what does the Great Universal Turtle stand on?"

The Sage replied, "These are very perceptive questions, mister, but they'll do you no good. It's turtles all the way down."

This is a good story to tell people who proclaim simplistic solutions to complex problems. They need to avoid the Turtle Syndrome. One particularly prevalent turtlish idea people too often entertain is this: Things are getting worse and worse, so we need to go back to the "good old days.'' These people should tape the following story to their fridge.

475. An Assyrian inscription, carved in stone, about 1500 B.C.: ''Our earth is degenerate in these latter days; there are signs that the world is speedily coming to an end; bribery and corruption are common; children no longer obey their parents; every man wants to write a book; indeed, the end of the world is approaching.''

And so we are coming very near the end of this book. Book? I hardly dare admit that I've written this one book—not to mention the forty-three other books I've written—for fear that I may hasten the end of the world or at least promote degeneracy!

Let me state my view plainly: I am convinced, if we citizens of the world can see our human condition with humor, we stay alive longer and live better. Can *all* tragedy be done away with? No. Be assured, there's no attainable formula for that, despite the views of a certain fifth grader.

476. A fifth-grade class was practicing for the school's annual Thanksgiving pageant. The teacher wanted to make sure that the meaning of it all was clear, so she asked them: ''Now, boys and girls, who can tell us why the Pilgrims came to America?''

A boy raised his hand and, when called upon, confidently declared: ''So they could worship in their own way and make other people do the same.''

No doubt you have observed that I admire what mere children—and they're not so mere—write. Therefore, you'll not be surprised that the last story in the book is a paragraph written by a child.

477. The following was written by a seventh grader in Newark, N.J., on an assigned subject, *What the Pilgrims Found*, that was part of a project by the Educational Testing Service to rate paragraphs on a five-point scale, taking into consideration topic sentence, supporting facts, conclusion, vocabulary, mechanics, etc. I had these criteria so strongly in mind that I was blinded to the fact that here was a kid cleverly making fun of a dull assignment, and I rated it very low. Only when others read it and laughed aloud, did I recognize its humor and sophisticated structure.

What the Pilgrims Found

The land was hilly and stony. Sometimes it was stony and hilly. The stones were useful for making millstones and milestones. The Indians sharpened them. Stones they used for scalping and other social purposes. The hills were useful to watch Indians from. The Indians sometimes got there first. Then the hills were useless. The winters in New England were long. The summers were short. In keeping with the seasons, long underwear was worn in the winter. They wore short underwear in the summer.

—The End—

May we all, no matter what sort of undergarments we wear, be pilgrims! Pilgrims are those who travel to a holy place. How do we know whether the place we find is holy? We can be sure that it is *not* holy unless it is filled with humor and laughter.

I hope this book will help you on your journey, and help you to help others.

—The End—

Index

B

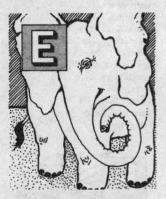

I take after my mother, 95
I watched my head, 117
ice cream, 60